An Anthology of Music in Early Florida

University Press of Florida

Gainesville · Tallahassee · Tampa · Boca Raton
Pensacola · Orlando · Miami · Jacksonville

An Anthology of
Music in Early Florida

Compiled and edited by **Wiley L. Housewright**

The University Press of Florida is the scholarly publishing agency for the State
University System of Florida, comprising Florida A & M University, Florida
Atlantic University, Florida International University, Florida State University,
University of Central Florida, University of Florida, University of North Florida,
University of South Florida, and University of West Florida.

University Press of Florida
15 Northwest 15th Street
Gainesville, FL 32611
http://nersp.nerdc.ufl.edu/~upf

To Riley, Kim, and Ross

Contents

CHAPTER 8. THE SOCIAL CIRCLE   149

CHAPTER 9. THE MEN IN GRAY AND THE FOLKS AT HOME 231

Preface

Much of the material in this volume has been drawn from extant collections of music assembled by Floridians of the nineteenth century. Sources also include diaries, official histories, letters, and other documents of the day. They put us in touch with our past, revealing the motives and sensibilities of natives and setttlers who came from four continents. They list the instruments played, and titles of songs. Images of their setting are described. The music itself tells of commitments, divisions, and coalescence of the societies they created. Our time frame spans the first three hundred or so years of Florida history.

The ceremonial music of native peoples of Florida was first described by military men who were sent to destroy what they considered a savage culture. Only later, during the Seminole Wars of the nineteenth century, did soldiers take the time to notate a few Seminole songs and dances. Not until the twentieth century did anthropologists and ethnologists undertake extended study of Creek and Seminole music. By then the vast bulk of the native population had been decimated by disease, wars, and removal to the west. The small enclaves that remained, however, continued to celebrate the ancestral holidays with rituals and songs and continued their character dances honoring Florida wildlife.

The Spanish began the main thrust of European settlement in Florida in 1565, bringing with them their nation's repertoire of music: Catholic plainsong, contrapuntal music for voices, graceful dances, *tientos* for vihuela, guitar, and organ. The remarkable *diferencias, fantasias, villancicos*, masses, motets, and dances of Spanish composers often demonstrated high formal achievement. The Spanish were also the first settlers on the east coast of North America to install a church organ.

While the French were only short-term settlers (from 1562 to 1565), they brought the first Protestant church music to Florida. They sang Huguenot psalm translations of Marot to music settings by Goudimel. They brought the first keyboard instrument, a spinet, to the east coast and also a small chamber orchestra. The Spanish troops destroyed the French colony in 1565, but not before the French had taught their psalms to the coastal natives. Chief Saturiba's men intoned those psalms to Dominique de Gorgues when he arrived in 1568 to avenge the defeat at Fort Caroline.

When the British acquired Florida in the Treaty of Paris in 1763, it took only a few months for the Spanish population to leave for Cuba, Spain, or Vera Cruz. The Spanish returned in 1784 and stayed until the transferal of Spanish Florida to the United States in 1821. This time, many Spanish families remained. British Florida extended to the Mississippi River and included the populations of Mobile, Natchez, and Baton Rouge. London initiated an aggressive recruitment campaign to entice persons of wealth and the second sons of well-to-do families to Florida. The British diversified the colony by bringing Greeks, Italians, and Minorcans to work on the Andrew Turnbull plantation. Equally important was the importation of a large number of African laborers, most of whom were slaves. Slave languages and dialects were aptly described as being as numerous as mosquitoes, and the music of these immigrants was just as diverse. The social life of whites revolved around British military men and their families. Soldiers sang their drinking songs and marched to traditional tunes played by small contingents of versatile musicians. With their families, they danced minuets and the country dances of Scotland. They sang small-scale arias from operas by such composers as the Arnes, father (Thomas Augustine) and son (Michael), and William Shield.

During the American Revolution, East Florida's population increased by 11,000, due largely to an influx of American Tories. These loyalists presented concerts and British plays, some of them with music. After the Revolution, land grants brought a steady flow of Americans into Florida from the north and west. They sang Scottish songs harmonized by Haydn and sea shanties that they themselves composed while loading cotton from Florida ports bound for Liverpool and Bristol. At church, they sang music by Handel, as edited by Lowell Mason, and fuging tunes by New England composers who were willing to ignore textbook rules when they got in the way of musical ideas.

Andrew Jackson became a hero of the War of 1812, although his treatment of both the Spanish and the Native Americans was inhumane. The English attempted to occupy ports of East Florida and Pensacola in 1813 but were defeated by American riflemen. Major General Andrew Jackson, commander of the seventh military district, and his troops drove the English from Pensacola and then moved to Mobile. There he made a plea to state governors to send volunteers to drive the English from New Orleans.

Sharpshooters came from the north in great numbers to overwhelm the aggressors. This victory made a hero of Andrew Jackson. Marches were composed, published, and played in his honor throughout the nation. Civilians sang new words to old British, Scottish, and Irish tunes celebrating the brilliant strategist of the War of 1812. Few knew that peace had been signed two weeks earlier.

The Seminole Wars seemed endless to infantry soldiers who battled Native Americans over territorial rights, officially as early as 1818. A second phase of the conflict began in 1835 and continued for seven years, and a third endured into the 1850s. The soldiers who came down from West Point to direct these wars, along with their multinational troops, brought music from the core European arts tradition, folk music, and an abundant assortment of sentimental songs. Also, more and more, as American citizens reached Florida, the taste in music coincided with that of the nation at large.

After Florida became a territory of the United States, it gradually grew in both population and wealth. In West Florida, citizens celebrated the carnival season and supported traveling theatrical companies performing tragedies, comedies, and farces, most of them from the English repertory. During intermissions, actors demonstrated their musical and dancing ability. Professional orchestras presented symphonies by Mozart and Haydn and piano pieces by Hummel, Gelinek, and Dussek. In Middle Florida, social life revolved around the plantation. House parties featuring piano playing and dancing were frequent. Professional pianists would come from such cities as Washington, D.C., Baltimore, Philadelphia, and Lexington to present their technically demanding repertoire. Singers performed songs that had been popularized by such stars as Jenny Lind and Maria Malibran. Professional theatrical companies brought to Pensacola the actress Ellen Tree and the comic Thomas Dartmouth Rice. The pianists especially favored opera transcriptions, fantasies, and variations. Love songs dominated among the singers. In East Florida, dancing dominated the social scene. The season between Christmas and Lent was a particularly active party time. Masked and costumed street-music celebrants filled the narrow streets in the days before Lent, and "posy dances" brought reluctant bachelors into the lively scene. Visitors agreed that the grace of St. Augustine's women could not be matched when they danced the "Spanish Dance."

The Civil War presented a dilemma for Floridians. Highly respected governor Richard Keith Call opposed secession and was supported by prominent unionists, but secessionists cast their economic and political future with the Confederacy. But secession and war did not silence Florida's musicians. The war did manage to mute the body of patriotic music that was familiar to all Floridians, and music for the new Confederate nation had to be written. When it was, it came to Florida with little delay. Publishers in Georgia, Virginia, the Carolinas, Alabama, and Louisiana published parodies of well-known traditional and patriotic songs and also heartfelt lyrics prompted by the tragedy of the war. These sad songs of war were sung around campfires and in parlors, and some of them were shared by partisans on both sides of the Mason and Dixon line.

Secular folk songs and dances were shared on festive occasions. Music of the church ritual was insular. Music was therefore both inclusive and exclusive. As populations grew during territorial days, political and economic exchanges among them became essential to their prosperity. Linkage in social and cultural life also became a part of the equation. The Civil War, while not unanimously approved in Florida, galvanized the population on a single issue of survival.

Americans had been forced together through political agreements, yet they were flexible enough to adjust to new conditions. In order for sparse Florida communities to survive, mutual respect among citizens was required. National heritages defined the cultures of the earliest settlers, including their taste in music. It may not be assumed that the cultures of the Spanish, French, British, Greek, Italian, and Minorcans evaporated as they were pushed in, out, and about Florida. Enclaves of each remained in the state as reminders of the old days and custodians of their cultures. It is remarkable that those who followed them staunchly respected the principle of a classless society and looked with favor on the rich diversity of music traditions. For many years Florida would have few composers of its own, but it energetically welcomed music of composers from other states, as a new component in the already rich repertoire. It was the music they came to know best.

I am grateful to my colleagues and students for studying and performing this music and to Regina Murphy and James Amend for typing the manuscript.

Chapter 1

The Native Americans

When William Hayne Simmons and John Lee Williams, commissioners appointed to select the site of a capital for the territory of Florida, met at an Indian village (now Tallahassee) in 1823 seeking a site for the capital of Florida, they were spectators at a ball game. The players were men and women of the Seminole nation, who were continuing an old and widespread custom of their Creek ancestors that was similar to games played by the Cherokee, Choctaw, and other nations. Music and dance had central functions in the ceremonies surrounding these games. The Seminoles preferred brief tunes, a text of few syllables, and choreography that evoked the spirit or the image of the dance. The song text counted for little. One Seminole declared, "White man's music talk too much." Anthropology professor Frank G. Speck was an early student of the ceremonial songs of the Creeks, and his 1911 version of the Ball Game Dance (No. 1) appears here. It was transcribed from a cylinder recording and is only one of many similar examples of dance music for this game. Tunes varied among the tribes, and mutations occurred over the years.

Ethan Allen Hitchcock, a musician as well as an effective army officer, was probably the first person to notate the music of Florida's fugitive Creeks. In the early 1840s he scored ceremonial songs he heard and dances he had seen. In 1916, Albert Gale notated other Seminole songs. Included here are the Quail Dance (No. 2), the Chicken Dance (No. 3), and the Hunting Dance (No. 4). His work was reported by Minnie Moore-Willson in 1928.

The most extended study of Seminole music was published in 1956 by Frances Densmore, ethnologist of the Smithsonian Institution. It contains not only multiple songs for the same event but describes such important occasions as the Green Corn Dance and the Hunting Dance. Due to the lack of extant music scores, the relation of this music to that of earlier periods cannot be determined. We quote these later examples because they conform to descriptions written by naturalist William Bartram and scenes painted by artist George Catlin. From the Densmore study, we include Corn Dance Song (No. 5).

The songs and dances have repetitive phrases, usually comprising only a few tones. The pentatonic scale is predominate. Rhythms are set in motion by a drum. Early descriptions suggest heterophony as a stylistic option. The pieces are invariably followed with a shout.

The Green Corn Festival was held in the spring after the corn was ripe. It has been described by historians as a religious rite, a thanksgiving for the corn that Florida Indians used in making bread. It began with fasting and cleansing of the body through the drinking of an emetic. On the day following, men of the tribe sang while dancing in a circle, then women joined the ceremony. The singing was accompanied by drums and rattles. In other ceremonies, a medicine man sang and gave advice on living a long life. The festival was described as lasting from three to eight days.

The Hunting Festival was held in the autumn, usually in October. It was a thanksgiving ceremony for success in finding meat to sustain the tribe through the winter months. Men hunted deer, turkey, and other game, which women prepared for feasting. The Snake Dance and the Horned Owl Dance were reserved for this festival. Dances such as those of the Snake, Chicken, or Alligator were choreographed to imitate the movements of the animals.

The English and Americans alike fought the natives of Florida, but when the battles were over, native poets and musicians remembered the savage treatment of their people, their enslavement, and their removal to the West. Osceola, the brave Florida warrior, typified the image of an American native hero. Tricked by a flag of truce, manacled and imprisoned, Osceola became the subject of a George Catlin portrait. "The Death of Osceola" (No. 6), a glee for four voices, was composed by B. F. Baker and published in 1846. Baker was a teacher, editor, composer, and singer in Boston. He succeeded Lowell Mason as superintendent of music instruction in the Boston public schools. S. S. Steele wrote the text. He evoked the image of Osceola as an "arrowed raven" wounded by falsehood. He used the sinking sun to symbolize Osceola awaiting death and reunion with his sires. A copy of this song is in the private library of Mark Fretwell of St. Augustine.

1. Ball Game Dance

tr. Frank G. Speck

Whoop

Repeat   eight   times

2. Quail Dance

tr. Albert Gale

Yah - ah   we   yah - ah   we - e   yah - ah   we   yah - ah   we

3. Chicken Dance

tr. Albert Gale

He yo-ho ta le ta le he yo-ho ta le ta le   he yo - ho   ta le ta le he yo - ho   ta le ta le

4. Hunting Dance Song

tr. Albert Gale

Twa yah ho - ta he   twa yah   ho - ta he   twa   ya ho   ta he   ah twa   el - lee

5. Corn Dance Song

tr. Frances Densmore

6. The Death of Osceola

S. S. Steele

B. F. Baker

Oh__ bring me the arrow'd__ ra - ven, That
I led__ my braves__ to bat - tle A -
He sent a sig - nal ban - ner White
E - ma - sas woods of flo - wers Now

I_ may send his plume,_ To_ tell_ my hun - ted na - tion Their
gainst the white man's pow - er, He_ felt_ our ar - rows rat - tle In_
as_ the young snow fleece,_ It_ spoke_ his pledge of ho - nor To
bear_ my death_ song far, To_ those_ blest spir - it bo - wers Where

fine   *energico*

fal - len chief - tain's doom.   The pan - ther of the pale - face Has
con - flicts go - ry hour;   He came with knives and thun - der I
light the pipe of peace;   We took his hand like bro - thers But
sinks day's gol - den star;   Ghosts of my migh - ty si - res I

lured me to his lair And the heart his fangs could ne - ver find, Is_
dug his sons a grave, He came with words of false - hood And
chains were in his clasp, And now my wrong'd soul smo - thers With -
seek your last free shore Where the white man's dea - thly fires can

break - ing in his snare.
now I am a slave.
in his i - ron grasp.
ne - ver hunt me more.

rallentando

D.C. al 𝄋

Chapter 2

The Spanish

During Cabeza de Vaca's 1528 exploration from Tampa to North Florida, he observed that Native Americans made therapeutic use of music in ceremonies similar to those of Spaniards. The Spanish healing ceremony was to make a sign of the cross, breathe on the subject, and chant a *Pater Noster* or an *Ave Maria* (No. 7). Later, when permanent settlements were built by the Spanish, priests taught the Florida natives to sing these prayers.

In 1559 a large company of Spaniards and their attendants sailed from Santa Cruz, New Spain, to a Gulf of Mexico port they called Ochuse. Today that port is known as Pensacola. After landing, Father Padre Martín de Feria, his four associate priests, and the company sang *Te Deum Laudamus* in gratitude for their safe arrival. Father Siguenza y Gongora, a lay priest, led a procession to a hastily erected cross. There the company knelt as he chanted the *Vexilla Regis* (No. 8), translated as "Forth comes the Standard of the King," which was appropriate to their missionary function. Later, on St. Mark's Day (April 25), the Spaniards sang the *Litany of Loreto* (No. 9), followed by a procession to the cross. This thirteenth-century litany is sung every evening in Loreto, Italy, in honor of the Virgin Mary. Here we quote only the Kyrie plainchant, which precedes the responsive line that is sung with the congregation. Following it, the intercession of Mary is invoked in forty-nine brief, descriptive variants.

In the retinue of Pedro Menéndez de Avilés (1565) were two fifers, drummers, three trumpeters, a harpist, players of the vihuela de arco, and psaltery. Six of his men were excellent singers. Small bands in Spanish St. Augustine and Pensacola played for parades and military exercises. Their forces were enlarged when they played for social occasions. We have no documentation concerning the music played at these military events. One Spanish source, however, includes military band and vocal music believed to have been played during the years of Spanish occupation. It is a collection ordered by Carlos III and published in Madrid in 1769. The pieces are scored for two fifes ("pifano" in Spanish), two clarinets, and drums. In 1939 they were arranged for the army of Generalissimo Francisco Franco. Two are included here: *La Generala* (No. 10) and *El Bando* (No. 11).

Diferencias sobre el "Canto del Cavallero" (Variations on the "Song of the Horseman"; No. 12) is from the large collection *Obras de musica para tecla, arpa, y vihuela* (Musical works for keyboard, harp, and vihuela) by Antonio de Cabezón. Cabezón (1510–1566) was one of the most illustrious early Spanish composers of organ music. We do not know that the early Florida organists played this piece, but it is an example of the mainstream literature from which Spanish organists of the period selected works for that instrument. It could also have been played on a spinet brought to Florida by the French, if that instrument survived the Spanish victory at Fort Caroline. It is the type of piece that was still in vogue during the twenty-year tenure of Don Antonio Ponce de León as organist at the cathedral in St. Augustine in the late seventeenth and early eighteenth centuries.

Aside from the professional musicians brought to Florida by Menéndez de Avilés, at least two privates in the army played the vihuela de arco and guitar. The music they played is not documented, but music for their instruments is contained in a well-known collection by the Valencian Luis de Milán, author of *El Maestro*. Two examples from this 1536 collection illustrate the genre and the style: "Al amor quiero vencer" (No. 13), and Pavan No. 4 (No. 14). They represent the type of music played by these instruments on social occasions of the period.

7. Ave Maria

A - ve Ma - ri - a, gra - ti - a ple - na, Do - mi - nus te - cum,

be - ne - dic - ta tu in mu - li - e - ri - bus, et be - ne - dic - tus fruc - tus ven - tris

tu - i Je - sus. Sanc - ta Ma - ri - a,

Ma - ter De - i, o - ra pro - no - bis pec - ca - to - ri - bus,

nunc et in ho - ra mor - tis nos - trae. A - men.

Hail Mary, full of grace, the Lord is with thee; blessed art thou among women, and blessed is the fruit of thy womb, Jesus. Holy Mary, Mother of God, pray for us sinners, now and in the hour of our death. Amen.

8. Vexilla Regis

1. Vex - i - la Re - gis prod - e - unt: Ful - get Crucis my - ste - ri - um,

Qui vi - ta mor - tem per - tu - lit, Et mor - te vi - tam pro - tu - lit.

2. Quae vul - ne - ra - ta lan - ce - ae Mu - cro - ne di - ro, cri -

mi - num Ut nos la - va - ret sor - di - bus, Ma - na vit un -

da et san - gui - ne. 3. Im - ple - ta sunt quae con - ci - nit

Dav - id fi - de - li car - mi - ne, Di - cen - do na - ti - o - ni - bus:

Reg - na - vit a lig - no De - us. 4. Ar - bor de - co - ra et

ful - gi - da, Or - na - ta Re - gis pur - pu - ra,

E - lec - ta dig - no sti - pi - te Tam san - cta mem - bra tan - ge - re.

5. Be - a - ta, cu - jus bra - chi - is Pre - ti - um pe - pen - dit sae - cu - li:

Sta - te - ra fa - cta cor - po - ris, Tu - lit - que prae - dam tar - ta - ri.

6. O Crux av - e, spes u - ni - ca, Hoc Pas - si - o - nis tem - po - re:
The 3rd May: Pa - scha - le quae fers gau - di - um(1)
The 14th Sept: In hac tri - um - phi

Pi - is a - dau - ge gra - ti - am, Re - is - que de - le cri - mi - na.

7.Te, fons sa - lu - tis Tri - ni - tas, Col - lau - det om - nis spi - ri - tus:

Qui - bus Cru - cis vic - to - ri - am Lar - gi - ris, ad -

de prae - mi - um. A - men.

1. Forth comes the Standard of the King: all hail the mystery adored!
Hail, Cross! on which the Life himself died, and by death, our life restored.
2. On which the Savior's holy side, rent open with a cruel spear, its stream of blood and water pour'd, to wash us from defilement clear.
3. O sacred wood! fulfill'd in thee was holy David's truthful lay; which told the world that from a tree the Lord should all the nations sway.
4. Most royally empurpled o'er, how beauteously thy stem doth shine! how glorious was its lot to touch those limbs so holy and divine!
5. Thrice blest, upon whose arms outstretch'd the Savior of the world reclined; balance sublime! upon whose beam was weighed the ransom of mankind.
6. Hail, Cross! thou only hope of man, hail on this holy Passion day! to saints increase the grace they have; from sinners purge their guilt away.
7. Salvation's fount, blest Trinity, be praise to thee through earth and skies: thou through the cross the victory dost give; oh give us too the prize!

9. The Litany of Loreto: Kyrie

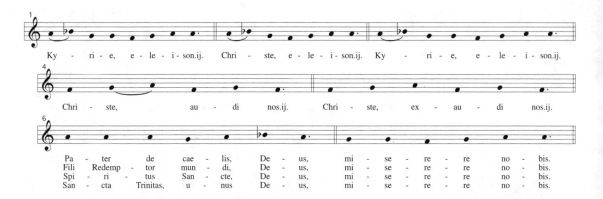

Ky - ri - e, e - le - i - son.ij. Chri - ste, e - le - i - son.ij. Ky - ri - e, e - le - i - son.ij.

Chri - ste, au - di nos.ij. Chri - ste, ex - au - di nos.ij.

Pa	-	ter	de	cae	- lis,	De	- us,	mi - se - re - re	no	- bis.
Fili	Redemp	- tor	mun	- di,		De	- us,	mi - se - re - re	no	- bis.
Spi	- ri	- tus	San	- cte,		De	- us,	mi - se - re - re	no	- bis.
San	- cta	Trinitas,	u	- nus		De	- us,	mi - se - re - re	no	- bis.

Lord, have mercy. Christ, have mercy. Lord, have mercy.
Christ, hear us. Christ graciously hear us.
God the Son, Redeemer of the world, have mercy on us.
God the Holy Ghost, have mercy on us.
Holy Trinity, one God, have mercy on us.

10. La Generala

Text by M. Tomás

Arr. by N. Otaño, S.J.

Ten - go fé en el des - per - tar de_Es - pa - ña: por si - glos y si - glos, an - te gente es - tra - ña,

siem - pre in - vic - ta - fué. Ten - go fé en el triun - fo_y la vic - to - ria, en un por - ve - nir de

glo - ria, her - ma - no del a - yer.

I have faith in the awakening of Spain;
for centuries and centuries, against foreigners,
she was always victorious.
I have faith in the triumph and the victory,
in a glorious future, brother of yesterday.

11. El Bando-Canción

Text by M. Tomás

Arr. by N. Otaño, S.J.

Quie - ro mar - char por la sen - da tri - un - fal ha - cia_el gran fi -
nal de_u - na au - ro - ra de glo - ria. Bus - co la vic - to - ria: la vic - to - ria_es - tá de - lan - te; ya no
mi ro pa - ra de - trás. trás.

12. Diferencias sobre el "Canto del Cavallero"

Antonio de Cabezón

13. Al amor quiero vencer

Luis Milán

14. Pavan No. 4

Trans. Charles Jacobs

Luis Milán

Chapter 3

The French

The Psalms of David became the basis for the music of the French Huguenots. John Calvin made metrical settings of five of them that were published in 1539 in Strasbourg. In that collection were twelve texts by the poet Clément Marot. A Geneva collection of 1542 contained thirty psalm-verses by Marot. Five years later, music settings by Louis Bourgeois appeared. They were largely adaptations of popular melodies.

Prominent among the Catholic musicians who were converted to Protestantism was Claude Goudimel. He did not write psalm tunes himself but made four-part settings of the melodies of Bourgeois, Guillaume le Franc, and others. He wrote psalm settings of words by Marot that were sung by the French en route to Florida. His first edition of such psalms, published in Paris in 1562, contained eighty-two selections. Two years later, it was expanded to include 150. In 1565 it was republished in both Paris and Geneva. The 1564 edition gave the melody to the soprano; the 1565 edition gave it to the tenor. Goudimel's harmonizations were simple, note-for-note settings intended for family devotions. At church services, Huguenots sang only the tunes. Goudimel's contrapuntal motets on the psalms, published between 1551 and 1566, were reserved for recreation or social worship.

The French settlers at Fort Caroline taught Florida natives to sing psalm settings from their services. Nicholas le Challeux, a carpenter of the colony, testified that the Native Americans sang Psalm 130 ("Du fons de ma pensée" [From the depths of my thought]; No. 15), and Psalm 137 ("Estans assis aux rives aquatiques de Babylon pleurions melancoliques" [Being seated on the banks of the river of Babylon, sad and weeping]; No. 16).

Another psalm that they sang gave assurance to all who accepted the faith that they would be rewarded with a comfortable and happy life in heaven. This was Psalm 128 ("Bien heureux est quiconques, sert à Dieu volontiers" [Blessed is whoever waits on God willingly and who never wearies of following in his ways]; No. 17).

Psalm 5 ("Aux paroles que je veux dire, plaise toi l'oreille prester" [To the words that I wish to speak, please give ear]; No. 18) was sung by both the French colony in Florida and the colony in Brazil in 1557.

Four Huguenot psalms are included here. It must be remembered that from one edition to the next, musicians made variants in the melodies, just as poets did in their metrical translations of the psalms. Some tunes served more than one text.

In addition to drums, fifes, trumpets, and French horns, the French brought a spinet to Florida. Aside from the organs built by Spanish priests in the southwest, it was the first keyboard instrument in what is now the United States and Canada. Its literature was collections of popular dances: *gaillardes, pavanes, branles,* and *basse danses.* It supported the social life of the colony, but no record was left of specific titles, composers, or publishers.

It may be speculated that one musician who was from La Rochelle sang ancient *chansons de marin* such as "Ce sont les filles de la Rochelle" and "En revenant de la joli Rochelle." Sailors from Brittany and Normandy probably knew "La Fille de la joli Rochelle," "La Fille á la fontaine," and "Ah! qui me passera la hois," popular songs in their provinces. Mothers of the eight or more children who were born in Fort Caroline may have sung such well-known children's songs as "Ah! vous dirai-je, maman?" "Sur le pont d'Avignon," "Au clair de la lune," and "Frere Jacques." All of these were known to French mothers of the period.

15. Psalm 130

Clément Marot

Claude Goudimel

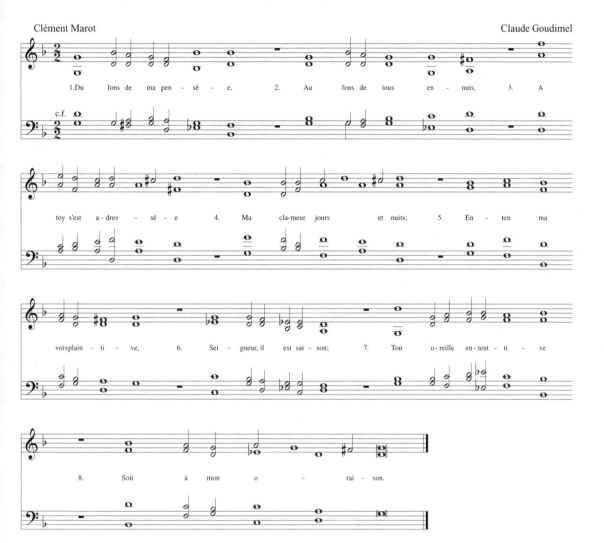

1.Du fons de ma pen - sé - e, 2. Au fons de tous en - nuis, 3. A toy s'est a - dres - sé - e 4. Ma cla-meur jours et nuits; 5. En - ten ma voix plain - ti - ve, 6. Sei - gneur, il est sai - son; 7. Ton o - reille en - tent - ti - ve 8. Soit à mon o - rai - son.

From the depths of my thought,
From the depths of all weariness,
To Thee is addressed my outcry day and night.
Listen to my plaintive voice, O Lord, it is time;
May your ear be attentive to my prayer.

16. Psalm 137

Clément Marot

Claude Goudimel

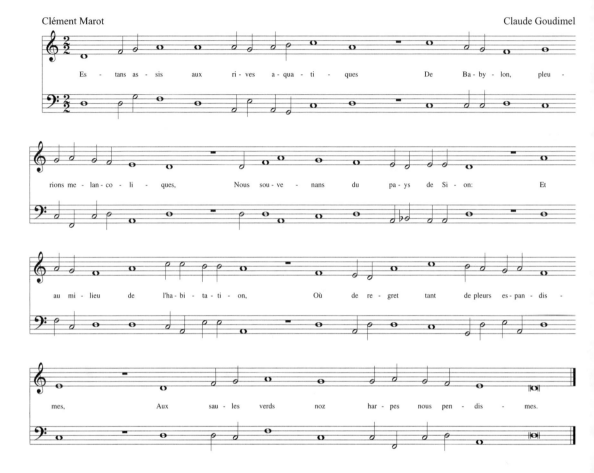

Es - tans as - sis aux ri - ves a - qua - ti - ques De Ba - by - lon, pleu -

rions me - lan - co - li - ques, Nous sou - ve - nans du pa - ys de Si - on: Et

au mi - lieu de l'ha - bi - ta - ti - on, Où de re - gret tant de pleurs es - pan - dis -

mes, Aux sau - les verds noz har - pes nous pen - dis - mes.

Being seated on the banks of the rivers of Babylon,
Sad and weeping, we, remembering the country of Zion
In the midst of the habitation,
Where on accounts of our regrets
We were shedding so many tears,
On the green willow we hung our harps.

17. Psalm 128

Clément Marot

Claude Goudimel

1.Bien heur- reux est qui con - ques 2.Sert à Dieu vo - lon - tiers 3.Et ne se las - sa on - ques 4.De sui - vre ses sen - tiers 5.Du la - beur que sais fai - re 6.Vi - vras com - mo - de - ment 7.Et i - ra ton af - fai - re 8.Bien et heur - reu - se - ment.

  Blessed is whoever waits on God willingly,
And who never wearies of following in his ways.
By the work that you know how to do
You will live comfortably,
And your affairs will go well and happily.

18. Psalm 5

Clément Marot   Claude Goudimel

1.Aux pa - ro - les que je veux di - re, re, 2. Plai - se toy l'au - reil -

le pres - ter, 3. Et à co - gnois - tre t'ar - res - ter 4. Pour -

quoy mon coeur pense et sous - pi - re, 5. Sou - ve - rain Si - re.

    To the words that I wish to speak, Please to give ear:
And stop (long enough) to learn
Why my heart thinks and longs,
O Sovereign Lord.

Chapter 4

The British

St. Augustine during the British years (1763–83) was first of all a military post. Some of the king's finest troops moved in and out of garrison in the small town. The rattle of fife and drums could be heard throughout the day. Bands composed of pairs of hautboys, clarinets, horns, and bassoons rehearsed three times a week and played for the usual military ceremonies during the day. Since musicians were required by contract to be "double-handed," they also played violin, violoncello, or other stringed instruments for evening social events. General James Grant's frequent dances and Masonic meetings assured them of employment and ample food and drink.

A popular air of the day was "The British Grenadiers." It was composed in the late seventeenth century and has served through many wars. For one British officer in the American Revolution, it was his solace when he became homesick. Another officer in a later war declared that his men liked it even though it sounded a little like a dunghill cock crowing. Two other instrumental pieces are considered by historians to be ancestors of this piece, one of the same title (1745) and a "Grenadiers March" (1685). The 1776 version of the "Grenadier's March" (No. 19) quoted here was popular during the American Revolution. Its source is a John Greenwood manuscript. John Greenwood was a fife major in the 15th Massachusetts Regiment during the American Revolution. He acquired a music manuscript book containing this 1776 "Grenadier's March" from a redcoat fifer. The tune is traditional, attributed to no composer. It is usually played as a quickstep, but at the Trooping of the Colour ceremony it is played at a slow tempo.

"Rule Britannia" was sung by both soldiers and sailors who came to Florida port towns. Originally written by Thomas Arne for the masque *Alfred*, it was printed as the end piece of his *Judgement of Paris* under the title "The Duke of York's March" (No. 20). John Philip Sousa wrote a setting for voice and instrumental elaboration to be played for British dignitaries who visited America (No. 21). A hundred years after its first performance in 1740, Florida maidens were playing Beethoven's variations on this theme (No. 22).

The slow cadence of Handel's "Dead March" from *Saul* (No. 23) was heard in Florida when the band and funeral cortege processed to the church. Handel was clearly the most important composer of the day, and selections from his operas and oratorios became popular favorites even in the colonies. John Bemrose, a British soldier in Florida, wrote on the hazards of ill-paired men marching to this funeral tune. In such collections as *Warlike Musick*, military bands of the time found marches from Handel's *Scipione*, *Judas Maccabeus*, *Rinaldo*, and other works.

James Oswald was a Scottish composer under the patronage of King George III. He became popular through the publication of his collections of Scottish songs, dance music, and incidental pieces for dramas. In America he was best known for the song "Roslin Castle" (No. 24). It appeared in several fife tutors and was published in America by G. Willig and E. Riley. It is a pastoral love song. Colin, a shepherd, on a spring morning sang a cheerful song of Nanny's charms. His song rang through the Scottish hills and echoed from Roslin Castle. He invited the muse to join in the song. Love shone through Nanny's eyes and filled Colin's soul with "sweet alarms." Nanny, then, was invited to come away with her swain. Curiously, the melody became a standard funeral march played by bands, and it retained that association from its early days in Florida. An exception was that it was played at a farewell banquet for General Andrew Jackson in Pensacola when he left his post as military governor. James Hewitt quoted it in his masque *The Battle of Trenton* (1797). It was, he wrote, an expression of grief of Americans for comrades killed in that battle.

Governor James Grant enlivened the social life of St. Augustine with dances, assemblies, concerts, and dramatic productions. The British colonists responded so enthusiastically that the governor judged them to be "Mason music and dansing mad." Minuets were the favorite dances. Their names were not recorded, but there are ample examples of the form from English sources of the period. D. and J. Rutherford published two volumes of a "compleat collection of the most celebrated minuets" in 1775–80, and from that collection we have selected three. The Royal Scots Regiment was stationed in St. Augustine in 1763, and it is likely that the soldiers danced to Scottish and English fiddle tunes, just as the queen of England does today.

"The Princess of Hess's Minuet" (No. 25) and "Lady Augustus Minuet" (No. 26) are formed of the usual two four-measure sections, each repeated. "The Duchess of Richmond's Minuet" (No. 27) is an exception to the usual form. It links two sixteen-measure minuets, the first in major, the other in minor. In the first, measures 13 and 14 are repeated, making a six-measure phrase. These are the prototypes of the minuets danced by the residents of the British colonies. Minuets were danced by couples in the early hours of the evening. They were followed by country dances in line or square formations. Cotillions, hornpipes, and reels were favorites. One reel was named for Balendalloch, the Scottish home of Governor James Grant. It was "Balendalloch's Dream" (No. 28), a lively tune.

The bachelor governor encouraged an active social life in St. Augustine. After serving about seven years in the colony, in 1771 he "sailed home to England, thoroughly pickled and gouty." An Irish reel, "Go to the Devel and Shake Yourself" (No. 29) was widely known among the early Florida Scots and also to later Florida fiddlers.

In 1666, Samuel Pepys declared Scots people pretty odd company. At a supper party, he heard Scottish tunes played on the violin and commented "but, Lord, the strangest ayre that ever I heard in my life, and all of one cast." He might have been astounded at the later popularity of the Scottish snap, and the appeal of the slow-tempo strathspey. That dance is represented here by "Marquis of Huntley's Strathspey" (No. 30).

Scottish and English fiddlers played lively tunes from a spate of publications. Directions for the dances were issued with the music score. "The Star" (No. 31) and "Shuter's Humour" (No. 32) are from a collection of country dances published in 1760 that was popular in Scotland and England. They were so widely distributed that they may have been known to the musicians and military men under General Grant's command.

Few eighteenth-century operas were performed in their entirety in Florida until about 1820 and thereafter. But many selections from the English repertory were heard in British territorial and statehood days. Among them were "Her Mouth, Which a Smile" (No. 33), from *Rosina* by William Shield; "This Cold, Flinty Heart" (No. 34), from *Cymon* by Michael Arne; and "Within This Breast the Record Lies" (No. 35), from Shield's *The Flitch of Bacon*. The first is a love song for baritone, while the other two are florid settings telling of how young ladies are won over. A violin duo performs an obbligato function in the last song.

Two bound collections of sheet music are believed to have been owned by a family that lived along the St. Johns River. Their dates are 1835 and 1836. Several of the songs in them were known by singers in the small towns along the Atlantic coast. Their titles were mentioned by writers of the British period and again by observers of the early-nineteenth-century social scene. One of them was "No, 'Twas Neither Shape Nor Feature" (No. 36), from William Shield's opera *The Flitch of Bacon*. As was the custom of the time, songs from several composers were included in an opera. J. C. Bach composed this song and it was published in London in 1778. Later, it appeared in a collection titled *The Beauties of Music and Poetry*, with the words "Gentle Breezes, waft him over."

19. Grenadier's March ca. 1776

Traditional

AN ANTHOLOGY OF MUSIC IN EARLY FLORIDA

20. The Duke of York's March

21. Rule Britannia

THOMAS AUGUSTINE ARNE,
arranged by
JOHN PHILIP SOUSA.

THOMSON & MALLET.

When Bri - tain first, at Heav'n's com - mand, a - rose from out the
The na - tions not so blest as thee, Must in their turn to

a - zure main, A - rose, a - rose, a - rose from out the a - zure main, This was the char - ter, the
ty - rants fall, Must in their turn to ty - rants fall; While thou shalt flou - rish, shall

3.

Still more majestic shalt thou rise,
 More dreadful from each foreign stroke;
As the loud blast, that tears the skies,
 Serves but to root thy native oak.
  Rule, Britannia! &c.

4.

Thee haughty tyrants ne'er shall tame;
 All their attempts to bend thee down,
Will but arouse thy gen'rous flame,
 To work *their* woe, and *thy* renown.
  Rule, Britannia! &c.

5.

To thee belongs the rural reign,
 Thy cities shall with commerce shine.
All thine, shall be the subject main,
 And ev'ry shore it circles, thine.
  Rule, Britannia! &c.

6.

The muses, still with freedom found,
 Shall to thy happy coast repair.
Blest Isle! with matchless beauty crown'd,
 And manly hearts to guard the fair.
  Rule, Britannia! &c.

22. Five Variations on Rule Britannia

Variation 1.

AN ANTHOLOGY OF MUSIC IN EARLY FLORIDA

23. Dead March from *Saul*

Georg Friedrich Handel.

24. Roslin Castle

RICHARD HEWIT.

The House of Glams,
Scots traditional Tune

'Twas in the sea - son of the year, When all things gay and sweet ap - pear, That
A - wake, sweet Muse! the breath - ing spring With rap - ture warms, a - wake and sing; A -

Co - lin, with the morn - ing ray, A - rose and sung his ru - ral lay: Of Nan - nie's charms the
wake and join the vo - cal throng, Who hail the morn - ing with a song! To Nan - nie raise the

shep - herd sung, The hills and dales with Nan - nie rung; While Ros - lin cas - tke
cheer - ful lay; Oh! bid her haste and come a - way: In sweet - est smiles her -

heard the swain, And ech - oed back the cheer - ful strain.
self a - dorn, And add new gra - ces to the morn.

O hark, my love! on every spray,
Each feathered warbler tunes his lay;
'Tis beauty fires the ravished throng,
And love inspires the melting song.
Then let my raptured notes arise,
For beauty darts from Nannie's eyes,
And love my rising bosom warms,
And fills my soul with sweet alarms.

O come, my love! thy Colin's lay
With rapture calls; O come away!
Come, while the Muse this wreath shall twine
Around that modest brow of thine.
O! hither haste, and with thee bring
That beauty, blooming like the spring,
Those graces that divinely shine,
And charm this ravished heart of mine!

25. The Princess of Hess's Minuet

26. Lady Augusta's Minuet

27. The Duchess of Richmond's Minuet

arranged by
JOHN RUTHERFORD.

28. Balendalloch's Dream

Reel

29. Go to the Devel and Shake Yourself

Irish Jig

This Tune may be played Slow.

AN ANTHOLOGY OF MUSIC IN EARLY FLORIDA

30. The Marquis of Huntley's Strathspey

WILLIAM MARSHALL.

31. The Star

Country Dance

The 1st Cu. cast off one Cu. Cast up again. Gallop down one Cu. and cast off. Right hand and left.

32. Shuter's Humour

Country Dance

First Cu. lead through 2nd. Cu. and cast up. 2nd Cu. lead through 1st Cu. and cast off.
1st man foot to 2nd. Woman and not turn 1st Woman do the same to 2nd. Man, then 1st
Cu. cast off one Cu. and turn. 1st Man foot to 2nd. Woman and not turn 1st Woman foot
to 2nd man and not turn right and left at top.

33. Her Mouth, Which a Smile

from *Rosina*

WILLIAM SHIELD.

AN ANTHOLOGY OF MUSIC IN EARLY FLORIDA

34. This Cold, Flinty Heart

from *CYMON*

MICHAEL ARNE.

The Frost nips the Bud, and the Rose cannot blow,
From Youth that is Frost-nipt no raptures can flow,
Elysium to him but a Desart will prove,
What's Life without Passion — sweet Passion of Love?

The Spring shou'd be warm, the young Season be gay,
Her Birds and her Flow'rets make blithesome sweet May,
Love blesses the Cottage, and sings thro' the Grove,
What's Life without Passion — sweet Passion of Love?

35. Within This Breast the Record Lies

from The Flitch of Bacon

WILLIAM SHIELD.

With - in this breast the re - cord lies, Of all the vows, the vows he made, His Lips but more His tell - tale eyes His in - most Soul be - tray'd:

How could I shun the plea - sing pain, When all my doubts were flown, Be - sides my blush - es told the Swain, my heart, my heart, my heart was not my own.

36. No, 'Twas Neither Shape Nor Feature

from The Flitch of Bacon

Chapter 5

Military Men and Patriots

The Seminole Wars brought many young West Point officers to Florida. Among the best of them was Ethan Allen Hitchcock. He served at Ft. King in Tampa in 1840, at Ft. Stansbury near Tallahassee in 1842, at Ft. Preston in 1843, and at Camp Wilkins near Ft. Jesup in 1845.

Hitchcock was a fine flutist and keen observer of the community scenes where he was assigned. In one of his manuscript books he notated Indian music that he heard the Creeks sing: three dance tunes, a love song, and a lament. They were published for the first time in my earlier book, *A History of Music and Dance in Florida* (1991).

Hitchcock also notated the dance music of Florida settlers. "The Spanish Dance" was popular throughout the state in the first half of the nineteenth century. It was described as slow and graceful, in the manner of a minuet. Several composers wrote music for it. The Hitchcock notation, made during the Seminole Wars, is in my *History of Music and Dance in Florida*.

The Indian councils held during the waning years of the Seminole Wars were conducted with stylized ceremonies. When the Eighth Army Infantry under Major General Alexander Macomb arrived at Fort Heillman (Garey's Ferry, Florida) on April 5, 1839, they were greeted by a canon salute. Then the Second Dragoon's band played "Hail to the Chief" (No. 37). This march and chorus was first heard in the melodramatic drama *The Lady of the Lake* by Sir Walter Scott. The music was by James Sanderson, an Englishman. It was first performed in New York in 1812 and became known as a boat song. It was played for the inauguration of Martin van Buren as president in 1837. Over the years it has been played by the Marine band on patriotic occasions. It has been associated with the appearance of our presidents at official and social occasions.

Of the many drinking songs sung by soldiers who fought in the Seminole Wars, "The Cruiskeen Lawn" (No. 38) was one of the most popular. Its title can be translated as "The Little Full Jug." It is from the Scottish-Irish tradition and sings of the happiness the little jug brings. One editor has called it a distant relative of "The Little Brown Jug." Foot soldier Bob Madden sang it on the evening he and his unit arrived at Ft. Pickens in 1846. A fellow soldier reported that in celebration of the end of their long journey from Boston, they "duly chorused," drank, joked, and laughed "until nearly tattoo."

Boreas was the figurehead with tousled hair and pursed lips representing the North wind on maps used by seamen. "Rude Boreas" (No. 39) is one of the many songs about sea storms and wrecked ships. It is a work song advising the crew of danger and directing them to their duty posts. The final verses tell how the crew will celebrate their survival. This song was also sung at Ft. Pickens by Bob Madden. According to an English soldier in his unit, Madden bawled it out "at the highest pitch of his voice."

Andrew Jackson assumed the position of first military governor of Florida in 1821. Elaborate ceremonies with music celebrated the takeover from Spain. Jackson had become a national hero for his victories in the War of 1812. He won special acclaim during the First Seminole War for his victory over the British at New Orleans. In his honor, composers wrote military marches. Among them was a piano duet by F. L. Able, published in Philadelphia by G. E. Blake. Able, of Savannah, Georgia, was a teacher of Lowell Mason when Mason was a bank clerk in Savannah. When Jackson became president, other composers wrote grand marches celebrating his election. J. T. Norton wrote "President Jackson's Grand March" (No. 40). It was published in Philadelphia by the composer and played by Florida pianists.

The Apalachicola newspaper reported in fulsome detail events of the Fourth of July 1844. Patriots formed a procession to the council house and there heard a reading of the Declaration of Independence. The service music included the hymn "Denmark" set to Isaac Watts's words "Before Jehovah's Awful Throne" (No. 41). At the mid-afternoon dinner, thirteen regular toasts and forty-two volunteer ones were proposed. Horse racing, gambling, and a grand ball followed. The reporter commented that the company left well pleased and in good spirits. No doubt. The version here is from the *Boston Handel and Haydn Society Collection of Church Music* (1822), a collection then in use by Episcopal churches in Apalachicola and Quincy. This same hymn was played by the Florida Fourth Infantry band and sung "full blast" at a serenade of their Confederate chaplain in early June 1861 in Apalachicola.

When Florida became a territory of the United States, the boundary between Florida and Alabama became a political issue. Pensacolans voiced their bias by setting new words to a familiar Scottish song. The song was called "Within a Mile of Edinburgh" (No. 42), but it was popularly known as "I Canna, Winna, Munna Marry Yet." In the little romance, Jenny refuses to yield to Jockey's advances until he proposes marriage. Floridians refused the Alabama boundary proposal with the words, "We love her as a sister, but we would not be wed," sung to the traditional tune accompanied by an orchestra. The instrumentation of the orchestra is not known. The version included here is scored for voice, harpsichord, and strings. The voice part is faithful to the original tune. Introductory and closing sections and the accompaniment have been added by Urbani.

In Florida in the 1820s, 1830s and 1840s, the Fourth of July was an occasion for military men and civilians alike to put into effect the democratic idea of a classless society. Ships in coastal ports displayed colors and fired salutes at sunrise. At gatherings in the morning, deeply felt patriotism and spirituality set the emotional tone for the day. The mood became secularized as the afternoon feasts were served. Many toasts were proposed and earnestly cheered. Each was followed with music played by bands or sung by diners.

At St. Joseph and Pensacola, captains of ships invited citizens to join celebrations aboard their vessels. St. Augustine's festivities continued throughout the day for one and all. "Landlord, Fill the Flowing Bowl" (No. 43) was sung on this occasion, just as it sometimes is on festive occasions today.

Jean Lafitte, the French pirate, made shipping a hazardous profession in the Gulf of Mexico in the years before the War of 1812. The British attempted to enlist his help in the war against America, but instead of accepting the offer, Lafitte notified American general Claiborne, who relayed the battle plan to General Jackson in Mobile. Jackson requested military assistance from southern governors, whose troops arrived only a few days before the crucial battle of New Orleans occurred. Among the largest contingents were the 2,256 sharpshooter woodsmen from Kentucky. Their victory over well-trained British army and marine forces brought fame to them and their commander.

Lyricists and musicians lost no time in honoring their heroes. Samuel Woodworth, poet and author, wrote an eight-verse ballad praising "The Hunters of Kentucky" (No. 44). It never achieved the popularity of Woodworth's "The Old Oaken Bucket," but it was known well enough to be included in Florida music collections.

At the completion of his brief tenure as military governor, Andrew Jackson was honored by the citizens of Pensacola with a farewell dinner. Among the numerous toasts was a customary one to the ladies. The music that followed was "Come, Haste to the Wedding" (No. 45). It is a paean to love, innocence, and marriage that was composed by T. Giordani and popularized in an English pantomime, *The Elopement* (1767). The author of the text is Richard Brinsley Sheridan. A Thomas Linley version appeared in London in 1775 under the title *The Duenna*. It was performed in New York in 1786 and Charleston in 1787 under that name. After the turn of the century, it was published by five American publishers. Two issued it under the title "Rural Felicity" as sets of variations for piano. One issued it under the original title as a fiddle tune for dancing.

37. Hail to the Chief

Sir Walter Scott

James Sanderson

Maestoso

Hail to the Chief who in tri - umph ad - van - ces! Hon - or'd and bless'd be the
Ours is no sap - ling, chance - sown by the foun - tain, Bloom - ing at Bel - tane, in
Row, vas - sals, row for the pride of the High - lands! Stretch to your oars, for the

ev - er - green Pine! Long may the tree, in his ban - ner that glan - ces,
win - ter to Fade; When the whirl - wind has stripp'd ev - 'ry leaf on the moun - tain, The
ev - er - green Pine! O, that the rose - bud that gra - ces yon is - lands, Were

Flour - ish, the shel - ter and grace of our line! Hail to the Chief who in tri - umph ad - van - ces,
more shall Clan - Al - pine ex - ult in her shade. Ours is no sap - ling, chance - sown by the foun - tain,
wreath'd in a gar - land a - round him to twine! Row, vas - sals, row, for the pride of the High - lands!

Hon - or'd and bless'd be the ev - er - green Pine! Long may the tree, in his
Bloom - ing at Bel - tane, in win - ter to fade, When the whirl - wind has stripp'd ev - 'ry
Stretch to your oars for the ev - er - green Pine! O, that the rose - bud that

ban - ner that glan - ces, Flour - ish, the shel - ter and grace of our line!
leaf on the Moun - tain, The more shall Clan - Al - pine ex - ult in her shade.
gra - ces yon is - lands, Were wreath'd in a gar - land a - round him to twine!

f Allegro

Heav'n send it hap - py dew, Earth lend its sap a - new; Gai - ly to bour - geon and
Moor'd in the rift - ed rock, proof to the Tem - pest shock, Firm - er he roots him, the
O, that some seed - ling gem, Wor - thy such no - ble stem, hon - or'd and bless'd in their

broad - ly to grow; While ev - 'ry High - land glen, Sends our shout back a - gain,
ru - der it blow; Men - tieth and Bread - al - bane, then, E - cho his praise a - gain,
sha - dow might grow! Loud should Clan - Al - pine then Ring from the deep - most glen,

"Rod - er - igh Vich Al - pine dhu, ho! i - e - roe!"

38. The Cruiskeen Lawn

WILLIAM COLE

NORMAN MONATH

Translation of the Chorus:
Little jug, my heart's love,
Bright health to my own dove;
Little jug my own heart's love, love, love,
Oh, Little jug my own heart's love!

2.

Immortal and divine,
Great Bacchus, god of wine,
   Create me by adoption thy son;
In hopes that you'll comply
That my glass shall ne'er run dry,
   Nor my smiling little cruiskeen lawn, lawn, lawn,
   My smiling little cruiskeen lawn.
Chorus:

3.

And when grim death appears,
After few but happy years,
   And tells me that my glass it has run;
I'll say, "Begone, ye knave!
For great Bacchus gave me leave,
   To drink another cruiskeen lawn, lawn, lawn,
   To drink another cruiskeen lawn.
Chorus:

4.

Then fill your glasses high,
Let's not part with lips a-dry,
   Though the lark now proclaims it is dawn;
And since we can't remain,
May we shortly meet again,
   To fill another cruiskeen lawn, lawn, lawn,
   To fill another cruiskeen lawn.
Chorus:

39. Rude Boreas

Come rude Bo-reas blust-'ring rai-ler List ye lands-men all to me,
Ship-mates hear a bro-ther sai-lor sing of the dan-gers of the sea. From bound-ing
bil-lows first in mo-tion, When the dis-tant whirl-winds rise, To the
tem-pest trou-bled o-cean, When the skies con-tend with skies.

Hark the bosun's hoarsely bawlin', by tops'l sheets an' halyards stand,
Down t'gans'ls quick be haulin', down yer stays'ls, hard, boys, hard!
See it freshens, set taut the braces, tops'ls sheets now let go,
Luff, boys, luff, don't make wry faces, up yer tops'ls nimbly clew.

O'er the ship the wild waves beatin', we for wives and children moan,
Alas from here there's no retreatin', alas, to them there's no return;
Still the leak is gainin' on us, both chain-pumps are jammed below,
Heaven have mercy here upon us, for only that can save us now.

All the while fierce thunder's roarin', peel on peel contendin' flash,
On our heads fierce rain falls pourin', in our eyes blue lightnings flash;
All around us one wide water, all above us one black sky,
Different deaths at once surround us, hark! what means that dreadful cry?

On the lee beam there is land, boys, let the guns overboard be thrown,
To the pump come every hand, boys, see the mizen mast is gone;
The leak we've found it can't pour faster, we've lightened her a foot or more,
Up an' rig a jury foremast, she's right, she's right, boys, we're offshore.

Now once more on shore we're thinkin', since kind Heaven has saved our lives,
Come the cup now let's be drinkin' to our sweethearts an' our wives;
Fill it up, about the ship wheel it, close to our lips a-brimmin' fine,
Where's the tempest, now, who feels it? None! the danger's drowned in wine!

40. President Jackson's Grand March

J.T. Norton

Trio Flauto

Finis

41. Before Jehovah's Awful Throne

Denmark

Isaac Watts

Dr. Madan

Be - fore Je - ho-vah's aw - ful throne, Ye na-tions bow with sa - cred joy!

Know that the Lord is God a - lone, He can cre - ate and he des - troy, He can cre - ate and

he des - troy. His sov' - reign pow'r, with - out our aid, Made us of clay, and

     AN ANTHOLOGY OF MUSIC IN EARLY FLORIDA

Vast as e - ter - ni - ty, e - ter - ni - ty thy love; Firm as a rock thy truth shall stand, When roll - ing

years shall cease to move, shall cease to move, When roll - ing years shall cease to

move, When roll - ing years shall cease to move.

42. Within a Mile of Edinburgh

Scots traditional,
arranged by PETER URBANI

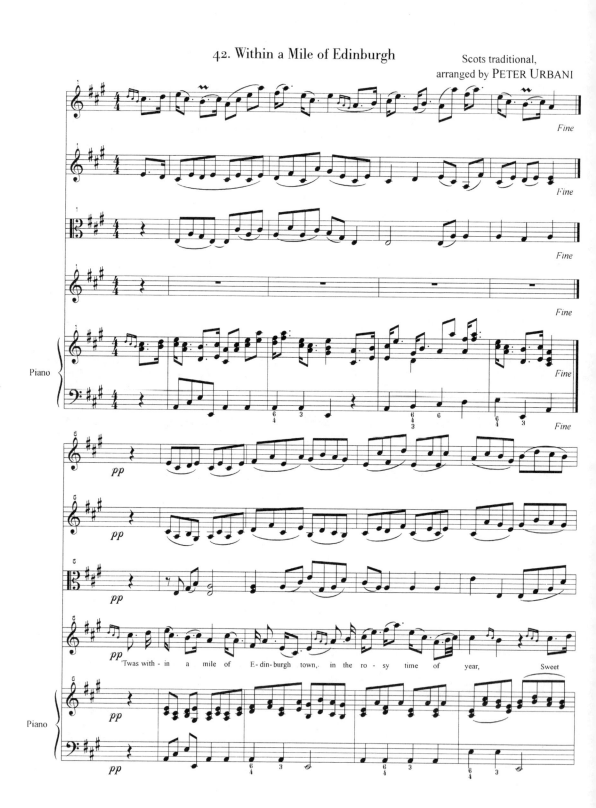

'Twas with-in a mile of E-din-burgh town, in the ro-sy time of year,   Sweet

Jocky was a wag that never would wed,
Tho' long he had follow'd the lass,
Contented she earn'd and eat her brown bread,
And merrily turn'd up the grass.
Bonny Jocky, blithe and free
Won her heart right merrily.
Yet still she blush'd and frowning cry'd No no, it will not do;
I cannot, cannot, wonnot, wonnot, mannot buckle too.

But when he vow'd he wou'd make her his Bride,
Tho' his flocks and herds were not few,
She gave him her hand and a kiss beside,
And vow'd she'd for ever be true.
Bonny Jocky, blithe and free,
Won her heart right merrily.
At Church she no more frowning cry'd No no, it will not do;
I cannot, cannot, wonnot, wonnot, mannot buckle too.

43. Landlord, Fill the Flowing Bowl

Scots, Irish, English
traditional

Come, Land-lord, fill the flow-ing bowl, Un-til it doth run o-ver, Come, Land-lord, fill the flow-ing bowl, Un-

til it doth run o - ver. For to-night we'll mer-ry, mer-ry be, For to-night we'll mer-ry, mer-ry be,

For to - night we'll mer - ry, mer - ry be, To - mor - row we'll be so - ber.

2.
The man who drinks good whiskey punch,
And goes to bed right mellow,
Lives as he ought to live,
And dies a jolly fellow.

3.
The man who drinks cold water pure,
And goes to bed quite sober,
Falls as the leaves do fall,
So rarely in October.

4.
But he who drinks just what he likes,
And getteth "half seas over,"
Will live until he dies, perhaps,
And then lies down in clover.

5.
The pretty girl that gets a kiss,
And goes and tells her mother,
Does a very foolish thing,
And don't deserve another.

44. The Hunters of Kentucky

Allegro

Samuel Woodworth

Ye gen-tle-men and la-dies fair, Who grace this fam-ous cit-y, Just lis-ten if you've time to spare, While I re-hearse a dit-ty; And for the op-por-tu-ni-ty Con-ceive your-selves quite luck-y, For 'tis not of-ten that you see a hun-ter from Ken-tuck-y.

Chorus

O Ken - tuck-y, the hunt-ers of Ken-tuck-y! O Ken - tuck-y, the hunt-ers of Ken-tuck-y!

45. Come, Haste to the Wedding

Richard Brinsley Sheridan

T. Giordani

Come, haste to the Wedding ye friends and ye neighbors, the lovers their bliss can no longer delay, forget all your sorrows, your cares and your labors, and let ev'ry heart beat with rapture today, Ye votaries all at-tend to my call come revel in pleasures that never can cloy, Come, see rural felicity which love and innocence ever enjoy

Mrs. Dorman
Let envy, let pride, let hate and ambition,
Still crowd to and beat at the breast of the great,
To such wretched passions we give no admission,
But leave them alone to the wise ones of state,
We boast of no wealth, but of contentment and health,
In mirth and in friendship our moments employ,
Come, see rural felicity which love and innocence ever enjoy.

Mrs. Scott
With reason we taste of each heart stirring pleasure,
With reason we drink of the full flowing bowl,
Are jocund and gay, but all within measure,
For fatal excess will enslave the free soul,
Come, come at our bidding to this happy wedding,
No care shall intrude here our bliss to annoy,
Come, see rural felicity which love and innocence ever enjoy.

Chapter 6

Congregations

An early strong proponent of European music in Florida was Pedro Menén-dez de Avilés, the great convoy commander who established a firm Spanish settlement in St. Augustine in 1565. The announced purpose of his coloni-zation was to spread the Catholic faith and convert people of the New World. Music was an important agent of that process. During the Spanish years, Catholic music was the dominant church music of Florida. Examples of that music are in Chapter 2.

The early Protestant music brought to Florida was metrical settings of the Psalms of David sung by French Huguenots in 1562 and 1564 at Fort Caroline. Examples are in Chapter 3. King George III never stated that he occupied Florida for religious purposes. During the British years, there was a perpetual shortage of Anglican priests and no Protestant church building in either St. Augustine or Pensacola. The Church of England prescribed the rite, but services were held in homes or public buildings. The church music repertoire of England at that time included psalms from the collections of Sternhold and Hopkins, Tate and Brady, and Isaac Watts's psalms and hymns. In Scotland, the Francis Rous psalm translations con-tinued to be used. Those tunes are similar to those of Goudimel and Bour-geois in the French Psalters. These were the sources of church music in British Florida.

During the territorial and early statehood period, homesteaders from the northern and western frontiers brought their hymns to Florida. Many of their collections borrowed liberally from Scottish and English sources. Others were edited by pious locals who introduced a generous sampling of American poetry and music and even new styles of music notation. The poetic hymns and psalms of Isaac Watts were staple offerings in both Florida and Great Britain. Some collections fused traditional doctrine to rural taste. Others sought to elevate taste. Hymns were sung everywhere: in church services, singing schools, social circles, and private devotions. For many, hymns were the only music they knew.

Early in the nineteenth century, publishers often printed the verses of the hymns without the tunes. In a process called "lining out," the minister or a church member would chant the phrases of the melodies, which were then responsively sung by the congregation. By the late eighteenth century, lining out had begun to fade in English parish churches, but it continues even today in some rural churches in Scotland and the United States.

Among the early collections printed with music notation available in Florida were *Mercer's Cluster* and the *Baptist Harmony*. They were oblong volumes that churchmen and music craftsmen composed, arranged, and assembled themselves, and they presented music for country folk—not the type of material cordially received by the urban congregations of the eastern seaboard.

The ever-increasing number of Baptist, Methodist, and Presbyterian communicants in rural Florida favored the *Sacred Harp*, assembled and edited by B. F. White and E. J. King in 1844. The book has gone through many editions and continues to serve loyal devotees of the tradition more than 150 years after it was first published.

Following New England models such as *The Easy Instructor* by William Smith and William Little and *The Christian Harmony* by Jeremiah Ingalls, White and King's *The Sacred Harp* used four shaped noteheads, retaining that method even after seven shapes became popular. Among the adaptations of folk tunes it included are "Wondrous Love" (No. 46) and "Amazing Grace" (No. 47). "When I Can Read My Title Clear" (No. 48) is an Isaac Watts hymn that was preferred by Methodists and Baptists. The text is an affirmation that the hope of heaven may support one through the trials of this earth. It reached Florida in two versions. One, in Thomas Hasting's *Sacred Songs for Family and Social Worship* (1842), was set to the tune "Medfield" by William Mather. The setting preferred by Floridans, however, was the tune "Pisgah," as in the version published in Joseph Funk's *New Harmonia Sacra* and in the *Sacred Harp*.

Gapped scales are used freely in these settings. The third and sixth scale tones are lowered in many pieces. Final chords at cadences sometimes omit the third. Open perfect fourths and fifths are characteristic of many harmonizations. *Sacred Harp* singers customarily sang the tunes with fa-sol-la syllables, then with words. Tenors usually sang the melody, sometimes doubled by the sopranos. This practice continues with some sacred harp singers today.

The fuging tune style that was to become a benchmark of many southern collections was brought to Florida by immigrants from the north. It came in many forms and is represented here by that New England icono-clastic champion of the idiom, William Billings, in his "Easter Anthem" (No. 49). Floridans sang it from the *Sacred Harp*.

Episcopal church choirs in Quincy and Apalachicola in the 1840s sang from the most widely distributed collection of church music in the nation, *The Boston Handel and Haydn Society Collection of Sacred Music* (1822), edited by Lowell Mason. It includes many hymns that continue to be sung by twentieth-century choirs. Among those are "Awake, My Soul, Stretch Every Nerve" (No. 50), by Handel; "Mighty God, Eternal Father" (No. 51), by Haydn; and "Come, Thou Almighty King" (No. 52), by Giardini. In each of these the melody is given to the tenors. The music for the Haydn title was adopted as the national hymn of Austria.

On the Wacissa plantation of Octavius N. Gadsen, slaves sang under the great oak tree of the estate. Among their songs was "A Great Camp-meetin' in de Promised Land" (No. 53), now better known by its first line, "Oh, walk together, children." The song advised children to talk, sing, shout, slap their hands, and pat their feet because there was a better day coming at a great camp meeting in the promised land.

Susan Bradford Eppes, diarist of early Tallahassee, has written that "I'm a-Rolling" (No. 54) was a favorite congregational song among African-American singers on the Tallahassee plantations. The singer is "a rolling thro' an unfriendly world," soliciting prayers and help from brothers, sisters, and preachers.

In 1865, a Boston journalist reported hearing the 200 African-American members of the non-segregated Fernandina Methodist church sing the spiritual "Good News, de Chariot's Comin'" (No. 55). The effect, he reported, was "absolutely thrilling" when the congregation improvised an appropriate verse in response to General Sherman's general order mandating humane treatment for freed slaves. The version here, in common use at the time, gives the lead line to a tenor. It was sometimes sung by a soprano.

Florida's African-Americans did not reserve their spirituals for church services and camp meetings. Many of their work songs were also spirituals. Cotton pickers at the Eppes farms sang "Mary and Martha" (No. 56). In the song, Mary and Martha are only the first "to ring those charming bells" in heaven. Others who follow are preachers, elders, fathers, mothers, Methodists, and Baptists.

46. Wondrous Love

Sacred Harp, 1844

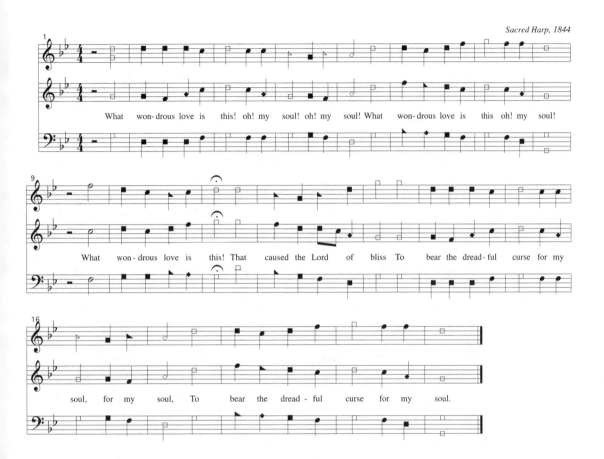

What won-drous love is this! oh! my soul! oh! my soul! What won-drous love is this oh! my soul!

What won-drous love is this! That caused the Lord of bliss To bear the dread-ful curse for my

soul, for my soul, To bear the dread-ful curse for my soul.

47. Amazing Grace

New Britain

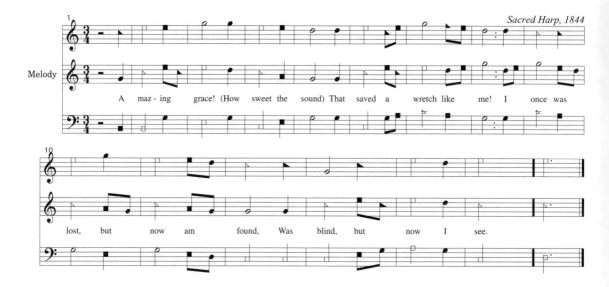

Melody

A maz - ing grace! (How sweet the sound) That saved a wretch like me! I once was lost, but now am found, Was blind, but now I see.

The earth shall soon dissolve like snow,
The sun forbear to shine;
But God, who call'd me here below,
Will be forever mine.

Through many dangers, toils, and snares,
I have already come;
'Tis grace has brought me safe thus far,
And grace will lead me home.

The Lord has promised good to me,
His word my hope secures;
He will my shield and portion be,
As long as life endures.

Yes, when this flesh and heart shall fail,
And mortal life shall cease,
I shall possess, within the veil,
A life of joy and peace.

The earth shall soon dissolve like snow,
The sun forbear to shine;
But God, who call'd me here below,
Will be forever mine.

48. When I Can Read My Title Clear

Pisgah.C.M.

Isaac Watts

Sacred Harp, 1844

When I can read my ti - tle clear To man - sions in the skies

I'll bid fare - well to eve - ry fear And wipe my weep - ing eyes, And

wipe my weep - ing eyes And wipe my weep - ing eyes; I'll

bid fare - well to eve - ry fear, And wipe my weep - ing eyes.

Should earth against my soul engage, and hellish darts be hurl'd,
Then I can smile at Satan's rage, And face a frowning world.

Let cares like a wild deluge come, And storms of sorrow fall,
May I safely reach my home, My God, my heav'n, my all.

49. Easter Anthem

from B. F. White and E. J. King's *Sacred Harp*

WILLIAM BILLINGS.

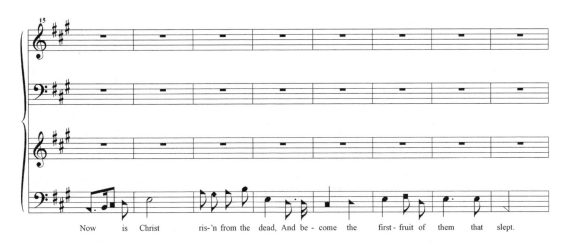

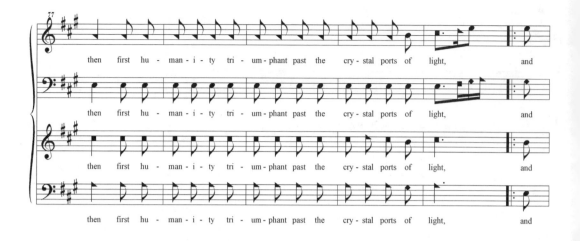

then first hu-man-i-ty tri-um-phant past the cry-stal ports of light, and

seiz'd e-ter-nal youth. youth. Man all im-mor-tal hail, hail, Hea-ven, all la-vish of strange gifts to man,

Thine's all the glo-ry, man's the bound-less bliss.

50. Awake, My Soul, Stretch Every Nerve

Arranged by LOWELL MASON.

GEORG FRIEDRICH HANDEL.

51. Mighty God, Eternal Father

arranged by
LOWELL MASON.

FRANZ JOSEF HAYDN.

Allegretto Maestoso.

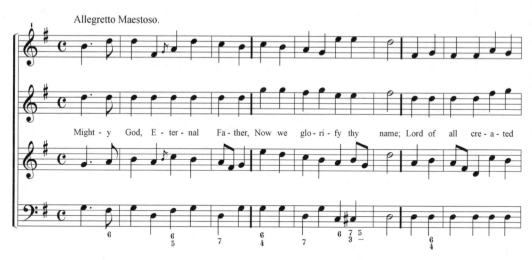

Might - y God, E - ter - nal Fa - ther, Now we glo - ri - fy thy name; Lord of all cre - a - ted

na - ture, Thou art ev-'ry crea-ture's theme— Hal - le - lu-jah! Hal - le - lu-jah! Hal - le - lu-jah! A - men!

52. Come, Thou Almighty King

arranged by
LOWELL MASON.

FELICE DE GIARDINI.

Come, thou Al - migh ty King, Help us thy name to sing, Help us to praise!

Fa - ther all glo - ri - ous, O'er all vic - to - ri - ous, Come and reign o - ver us, An - cient of days!

53. A Great Camp-meetin' in de Promised Land

Spiritual, arranged by
Mrs. M. F. ARMSTRONG
& HELEN LUDLOW

2.

Oh get you ready children, Don't you get weary,
Get you ready childron, Don't you get weary (*bis.*),
Dere's a great camp-meetin' in de Promised Land.
For Jesus is a comin', Don't you get weary,
Jesus is a comin', Don't you get weary (*bis.*),
Dere's a great camp-meetin' in de Promised Land.
Gwine to hab a happy meetin', Don't you get weary,
Hab a happy meetin', Don't you get weary (*bis.*),
Dere's a great camp-meetin' in de Promised Land.
CHO.—Gwine to pray an' nebber tire,
      Pray an' nebber tire (*bis.*),
      Dere's a great camp-meetin' in de Promised Land.

3.

Gwine to hab it in hebben, Don't you get weary,
Gwine to hab it in hebben, Don't you get weary (*bis.*),
Dere's a great camp-meetin' in de Promised Land.
Gwine to shout in hebben, Don't you get weary,
Shout in hebben, Don't you get weary (*bis.*),
Dere's a great camp-meetin' in de Promised Land.
Oh will you go wid me, Don't you get weary,
Will you go wid me, Don't you get weary (*bis.*),
Dere's a great camp-meetin' in de Promised Land.
CHO.—Gwine to shout an' nebber tire,
      Shout an' nebber tire (*bis.*),
      Dere's a great camp-meetin' in de Promised Land.

4.

Dere's a better day comin', Don't you get weary,
Better day a comin', Don't you get weary (*bis.*),
Dere's a great camp-meetin' in de Promised Land.
Oh slap your hands children, Don't you get weary,
Slap your hands children, Don't you get weary (*bis.*),
Dere's a great camp-meetin' in de Promised Land.
Oh, put your foot children, Don't you get weary,
Put your foot childron, Don't you get weary (*bis.*),
Dere's a great camp-meetin' in de Promised Land.
CHO.—Gwine to live wid God forever,
      Live wid God forever (*bis.*),
      Dere's a great camp-meetin' in de Promised Land.

5.

Oh, feel de Spirit a movin', Don't you get weary,
Feel de Spirit a movin', Don't you get weary (*bis.*),
Dere's a great camp-meetin' in de Promised Land.
Oh, now I'm gettin' happy, Don't you get weary,
Now I'm gettin' happy, Don't you get weary (*bis.*),
Dere's a great camp-meetin' in de Promised Land.
I feel so happy, Don't you get weary,
Feel so happy, Don't you get weary (*bis.*),
Dere's a great camp-meetin' in de Promised Land.
CHO.—Oh, fly an' nebber tire,
      Fly an' nebber tire (*bis.*),
      Dere's a great camp-meetin' in de Promised Land.

54. I'm a-Rolling

arr. T.F. Seward

I'm a roll-ing, I'm a roll-ing, I'm a roll-ing thro' an un-friend-ly world, I'm a roll-ing, I'm a

roll-ing thro' an un-friend-ly world. O bro-thers,* won't you help me O bro-thers won't you

help me to pray? O bro-thers won't you help me, Won't you help me in the ser-vice of the Lord?

*sisters
preachers

55. Good News, de Chariot's Comin'

Spiritual. arranged by
T. F. SEWARD

2. Dar's a long white robe in de hebben, I know,
A long white robe in de hebben, I know,
A long white robe in de hebben, I know,
An' I don' want her leave-a me behind.
Dar's a golden crown in de hebben, I know,
A golden crown in de hebben, I know,
A golden crown in de hebben, I know,
An' I don' want her leave-a me behind.
CHO.—Good news, de chariot's comin', &c.

3. Dar's a golden harp in de hebben, I know,
A golden harp in de hebben, I know,
A golden harp in de hebben, I know,
An' I don' want her leave-a me behind.
Dar's silver slippers in de hebben, I know,
Silver slippers in de hebben, I know,
Silver slippers in de hebben, I know,
An' I don' want her leave-a me behind.
CHO.—Good news, de chariot's comin', &c.

56. Mary and Martha

Arr. T. F. Seward

Ma-ry and a Mar-tha's just gone 'long, Ma-ry and a Mar-tha's just gone long, Ma-ry and a Mar-tha's

just gone 'long, To ring those charm-ing bells; Cry - ing free grace and dy-ing love. Free grace and

dy-ing love, Free grace and dy-ing love, To ring those charm-ing bells. Oh! way o - ver Jor-dan, Lord,

Way o - ver Jor-dan, Lord, Way o - ver Jor-dan, Lord, To ring those charm - ing bells.

The preacher and the elder's just gone long,
To ring those charming bells.

My father and mother's just gone 'long,
To ring those charming bells.

The Methodist's and Baptist's just gone
'long,
To ring those charming bells.

Chapter 7

Folk Singers and Dancers

In the first published collection of slave songs in the United States (1867), William Francis Allen wrote, "The favorite of them, 'Roll Jordan, Roll,' is sung in Florida." Men of the First Light Battery, Connecticut Volunteers, heard Florida African-American singers sing this spiritual (No. 57) at a church meeting during the Civil War. The texts of these two early versions are almost identical. The melody fits both texts very well. In the many later versions, a new tune retains the distinctive lowered seventh scale tone. The words carry an elevated revival message. The best-known a cappella version of the late nineteenth century was that of the Fisk University Jubilee Singers. J. Rosamond Johnson, a talented African-American composer from Jacksonville, arranged that version by adding a piano accompaniment, which he dedicated to Paul Robeson. That is the version included here.

Songs that African Bahamians brought to Key West mixed religion and social life. A few verses were traditional, and others were improvised. "Didn't It Rain, My Elder" (No. 58) is a retelling of the story of Noah's flood with reference to familiar locales.

The first verse of "Git on Board" (No. 59) invites all children to get on board a heavenly train. The second extends an invitation to sinners to board a ship crewed by Jesus and angels. The vocabulary and vocal practices of the African Bahamians differed only a little from those of African Americans. Their dominant religious beliefs stemmed from Anglo-Protestantism, as did many of their spirituals. In both the Bahamas and Key West, one singer "lined up" phrases of the hymns and others responded. African Americans "lined out," as did their white counterparts. Bahamians called one of their all-night songfests a "settin' up."

Many Florida slaves were given time off on weekends, which they often used for singing and dancing. These country parties or celebrations were called "frolics" and were a time for improvising new steps to old tunes or for inventing catchy new tunes and steps. In Jefferson and Leon counties in the 1820s, a favorite step was "Cut the Pigeon Wing." It was an arm-flapping, high-stepping caper that imitated the mannerisms of the bird. At the

Folsom plantation, the dance was set to the music of "Sich a Gitting Up Stairs" (No. 60). It was introduced to minstrel show audiences by blackface performer Thomas Dartmouth Rice, and in the 1830s was published in Baltimore by G. Willig, Jr.

Charles Grobe, a German pianist, came to the United States in about 1839 and taught in colleges in Delaware and New Jersey. He became one of the most prolific composers in America and a very influential piano teacher. Many of his compositions—variations on opera themes, dances, and sentimental songs—were written for his students. An example is his *Favorite Melodies* series published in Boston by Oliver Ditson in 1852. It is arranged for four hands and contains three schottisches, three polkas, a waltz, and four sentimental songs. It also includes the African-American spiritual "Jordan Am a Hard Road to Travel" (No. 61). This work is in a bound volume formerly owned by Mary Laura Call, youngest daughter of Richard Keith Call, third and fifth territorial governor of Florida. It is now in the archives of Florida Agricultural and Mechanical University. The composer was a unionist. Governor Call opposed disunion. LeRoy Collins, governor of Florida from 1955 to 1961, was a strong proponent of civil rights for all citizens. His wife, Mary Call Collins, is the great-granddaughter of Richard Keith Call.

One Florida historian has written, "These frontier folk were far better learned in old British and early American ballads than their present day descendants and frequently sang with great gusto *Lord Randal, The House Carpenter, Lord Thomas and Fair Ellen, Two Loving Sisters Neat and Trim, Barbara Allen, Sweet Mary, The Rake and Rambling Boy* and *Maggie.*" To this list must be added Sir Walter Scott's "*Jock O'Hazeldean*" (No. 62) and "*My Boy Tammy*" (No. 63), which Col. Robert Butler sang at his annual Feast of Roses ball.

As with other ballads, these appear in many versions and with numerous accompaniments. Col. Butler probably sang without accompaniment. His favorite songs appear in the sheet music collections of Mary H. Haynes and other musicians of mid-nineteenth-century Florida. Col. Butler served in the War of 1812 and was appointed surveyor general of Florida in 1824. He entertained friends at his large plantation just north of Tallahassee.

"The Birks of Invermay" (No. 64) is a touching song that reminds Amanda that the rapture of young love is like a spring morning to be enjoyed, and that when age, life's winter, appears, she and her husband will decay among the birch trees of Invermay. This Scottish folk song was harmonized by

Haydn and Pleyel and set for two violins, viola, voice, and harpsichord by Peter Urbani. It was sung in *The Duenna*, an opera by Thomas Linley, in 1775. Along with other Scottish songs, it was also sung throughout Florida in the early years of the nineteenth century.

The music of Franz Joseph Haydn was played and sung in early Florida. The Whitfield family, which arrived in Tallahassee in the early nineteenth century, owned a four-volume collection of Scottish airs that included songs harmonized by Haydn. "Good Night and Joy Be Wi' Ye" (No. 65) was one of them. It is not unlikely that this tune served the "Good Night Ladies" function at Scottish governor James Grant's dinner dances in eighteenth-century St. Augustine.

Samuel Pepys wrote on January 2, 1666, that he had heard an actress sing "Barbara Allan" (No. 66). Bernard Bronson included 198 versions of it in his *Traditional Tunes of the Child Ballads*. Cecil Sharp found twenty-seven versions, and Alton Morris included four in his *Folksongs of Florida* (1950). The early versions are in English, but Scottish versions of the text appeared in Allen Ramsay's *Tea Table Miscellany* (1724–40). Florida settlers brought versions they had heard in Virginia, the Carolinas, Georgia, and Alabama. The ballad has become the most popular folksong of all time. Haydn himself wrote two versions, one in aid of the financially distressed Scottish publisher William Napier. It appeared in *A Selection of Original Scots Song* (1790–92). A later version appeared in George Thompson's *A Select Collection of Original Scottish Airs* (1799–1805), which was brought to Tallahassee early in the nineteenth century by the Whitfield family.

Displaced persons throughout history have sung songs of home. "The Exile of Erin" (No. 67) recalls the shady bowers of the exile's homeland and his family and friends. His dying wish is to return to hear the "harp-striking bards sing aloud with devotion, Oh! Erin, mavourneen! Erin go bragh!" The lyrics were written by Thomas Moore and set to the very old Irish air "Savourneen Deelish." In Florida, the tune was also sung around campfires by military men during the Seminole Wars. The preferred arrangement was for three voices set by John Stevenson.

The invention of the spinning frame, the spinning jenny, and the power loom sped the growth of cotton textile manufacture in Britain. Cotton grown and ginned in Florida and other Gulf states supplied the raw material. Sailing ships, then steamships, loaded at Mobile, Pensacola, Apalachicola, and St. Marks, bound for Liverpool and Bristol. The trade was very active. In 1860, more than 65,000 bales of cotton were produced for export from Florida ports. The men who loaded (and sometimes overloaded) these ships came from almost every port engaged in international maritime trade. They were Irish, English, Canadian, African American, and of other origins.

Just as sailors sang halyards to accompany their tasks at sea, they improvised chanteys as they heaved at large mechanical screws to pack cotton bales below deck in port. "Roll the Cotton Down" (No. 68) is a good example of the genre. The choruses of these types of songs were usually made up of a repeated line. The verses told stories about ports, crises at sea, the shipping-line clippers, and the girls who struck the sailors' fancy.

Many early chanteys came from the Irish, but as crews became multicultural, so did the chanteys. There were German, Australian, and Canadian versions, and along Gulf Coast ports the versions of African-American sailors added a new dimension. Lines from other folk tunes were interpolated whether they made sense or not. Logic was rarely as important as the right rhythm. There would be little reason, for instance, to have to "clear away the track, let the Bull-gine run" ("Clear the Track"; No. 69) at sea, but the interpolation stuck. Similar chantey-gang cotton-packing songs were sung by wharf gangs in Savannah and other southern ports. "John, Come Tell Us As We Haul Away" (No. 70) was a shore adventure story told by two shantymen, the first asking questions, the second responding. Two-measure phrases alternate between soloist and chorus as a shore-leave romance unfolds.

Christmas Eve was celebrated at Pine Hill Plantation with festive dances. Susan Bradford Eppes, daughter and granddaughter of prominent Tallahassee families, vividly described such a scene, naming ten tunes and describing the tempos and styles of each. A favorite was "Sir Roger de Coverley" (No. 71), an English dance similar to the Scottish reels, though a bit more stately in style and slower of tempo in the first two sections. The last section became the jig "Irish Washerwoman." Well-to-do Tallahassee families of the 1850s became acquainted with the fictitious Sir Roger as he appeared in Addison and Steele's *Spectator*. For many generations thereafter, they danced to the tune that bore his name.

Dancing was a component of life in Florida from early days as there were few social constraints against such entertainment. Diarists wrote of dancing among the Native Americans, and the Spanish and French settlers. Dances to traditional Scottish, English, and Irish fiddle tunes were popular during the British period. In Florida, the fiddlers and banjoists were usually African American. Colonel Robert Butler, adjutant to General Andrew

Jackson, once commented with pride that slave fiddlers were reared on his Tallahassee plantation. He added that he preferred a good breakdown to Italian music. At a Christmas party, Susan Bradford Eppes and her friends danced to "The Forked Deer" (No. 72) and "Fisher's Hornpipe" (No. 73). "Leather Breeches" (No. 74) was a favorite tune of Colonel Butler's. Even the old Scottish song, "Come Haste to the Wedding" was put into service. Susan Bradford Eppes wrote of social life in Tallahassee in her book *Some Eventful Years*, published in 1845. She also wrote a poem describing "Christmas Eve at Pine Hill Plantation." In it she names dance tunes that her mother played on the piano.

As pianos appeared on the scene, they often replaced fiddles, and music repertory for dance expanded to include marches, minstrel tunes, and themes from operas. The country dances, however, never lost their appeal. Young cracker sports even expanded the already considerable repertory by devising distinctive steps and giving them whimsical names. The music was required only to be functional.

"Green Gravel" (Nos. 75a and 75b), a singing game, was known throughout Florida by young African-American children who had learned it from English settlers. It is a very old song, and because it was transmitted orally, it has appeared in a great many versions. Interpretations of its meaning are equally numerous. In one version, the green gravel was thought to refer to the green grass surrounding a grave. The singer's head was turned in respect for the dead, and attendants walked backward when leaving the body. In several versions the game ended when the king's message was delivered, symbolizing communion with the dead. In one American version, the lover is found to be alive.

There are about as many tunes to "Green Gravel" as there are versions of the text. One of the early versions was sung in the Gaston district of Manchester in about 1835 (No. 75a). Its tragic ending may be compared to the early Florida happy ending (No. 75b). The tune may be contrasted to the simpler melody sung by Florida children a few years later.

As Irishmen loaded timber on English droghers in Mobile in the 1840s, they sang "Shule Agra" ("Come My Love"; No. 76). It is a love song sung by a girl as her boyfriend leaves for military duty. The tune was so appealing that crewmen and dock workers devised new versions of the story that declared devotion to distant sweethearts. The Irish continued to sing the traditional version.

In 1840 the editor of the *St. Joseph Times* attended an opera performance in New York and found it to be "studied, artificial, and unnatural."

As was the custom of the time, a well-known familiar song was sung at the interval. The song that night was "Robin Adair" (No. 77). The editor found it "fresh, artless, and unrestrained." He swore off attending opera, opting for simple songs that played on his heart strings. His sentiment was shared by many Floridians, though there were pockets of music lovers whose taste was cosmopolitan, even in towns as small as St. Joseph.

English and Irish sailors began singing "The Girl I Left Behind Me" (No. 78) in about the middle of the eighteenth century. Others picked it up and made it one of the most popular songs of the nineteenth and early twentieth centuries. Published in both England and America, it was played by military bands and sung in parlors. In Florida, it was among the favorite selections played at cotillions. Susan Bradford Eppes was apprehensive as she heard Tallahassee boys singing the song as they marched off to the Civil War. Florida's Confederate soldiers camped on the banks of the Rappahannock River sang it to lift their spirits. J. C. Viereck arranged the version included here, which was published by J. C. Schreiner and Son between 1861 and 1865 in Macon and Savannah, Georgia. It focuses on a soldier's prayer to return safely to his girl and is as much a love song as a marching song.

57. Roll Jordan, Roll

arranged by
J. Rosamond Johnson

To Paul Robeson

Roll Jordan, roll, Roll Jordan, roll, I want-er go to heav-'n when I die, To hear ol' Jordan roll. O, breth-er-en, Roll Jordan, roll,
O, sist-er-en,
Roll Jordan, roll, I want-er go to heav-'n when I die, To

hear ol' Jor-dan roll. Oh, broth-ers you ought - er been dere, Yes my Lord A-
sin-ner you ought - er been dere,

sit-tin' up in de king-dom, To hear ol' Jor-dan roll. Sing it ov-ah, Oh, roll. O,

Roll Jor-dan, roll, Roll Jor-dan, roll, I

want-er go to heav-'n when I die, To hear ol' Jor-dan roll.

58. Didn't It Rain, My Elder

Bahamian - arr. C.L. Edwards

Didn't it rain, my el - der, Didn't it rain, good Lord, Didn't it rain for - ty days. For - ty days an' for - ty nights, Lord, didn't it rain for - ty days.

Didn't it rain, Great Sestern,
Didn't it rain to Key West too,
Didn't it rain forty days.
Chorus.

Didn't it rain, my Leader,
Didn't it rain to Rocky Bay too,
Didn't it rain forty days.
Chorus.

59. Git on Board

Bahamian - arr. C.L. Edwards

Git on board, lit-tle chil-drun, git on bo'd, lit-tle chil-drun, git on bo'd, lit-tle chil-drun, It's

room fah ma-ny a mo'o. Says No-ah, En-och, an' E - li - jah, Lord, and all the Pro-phets too, No

sec-ond class on bo'd de train, No diff-ren' in de fare.

Git on board, ye swearers, git on bo'd, ye rum drinkers,
Git on bo'd ye backsliders, There's room fah many a mo'o.
The gospel sails are histed, King Jesus is de crew,
Bright angels is de captain, Lawd, and that's a heavenly crew.

60. Sich a Gitting Up Stairs

Minstrel Dance Tune

On a Sus-ke-han-na raft I come down de bay, And I danced and I fro-lick'd, and
fid-dled all de way, Sich a git-ting up stairs I nev-er did see, Sich a git-ting up stairs I nev-er did see.

2. Trike he toe an heel — cut de pigeon wing,
Scratch gravel, slap de foot — dat's just de ting.
   Sich a gitting up stairs &c.

3. I went to de play, and I see'd Jim Crow,
Oh! nigger Isam den he swell, for Jim was no go!
   Sich a gitting up stairs &c.

4. I look him in de face until I make him grin,
And den I trow a backa quid an' hit him on de chin.
   Sich a gitting up stairs &c.

5. Oh! I is dat boy know how to preach a sarmont
Bout Temperance and *seven up* an all dat kind of varmint,
   Sich a gitting up stairs &c.

6. Nigger hold a meeting about de Clonization,
An dere I spoke a speech about Amalgamation!
   Sich a gitting up stairs &c.

7. To Washington I go dare I cut a swell,
Cleaning gemmen's boots and ringin auction bell,
   Sich a gitting up stairs &c.

8. I call on yeller Sal dat trade in sausages,
An dare I met big Joe, which make my dander ris.
   Sich a gitting up stairs &c.

9. Says I "you see dat door? Just mosey, niggir Joe,"
Form I'm a Suskyhanner boy what knows a ting
      or two;
   Sich a gitting up stairs &c.

10. An den I show my science — prenez gardez
      vouz,
Bung he eye, break he shin, split de nose in two.
   Sich a gitting up stairs &c.

11. Sal holler out — den she jump between us,
But guess he no forget de day when Isam show
      his genus,
   Sich a gitting up stairs &c.

12. Den Big Joe went out, he gwoin to take de law,
But he no fool de Possum — I cut stick for
      Baltimore.
   Sich a gitting up stairs &c.

61. Jordan Am a Hard Road to Travel

arranged by
CHARLES GROBE

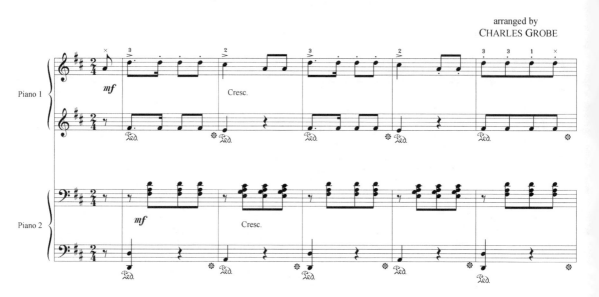

Piano 1

Piano 2

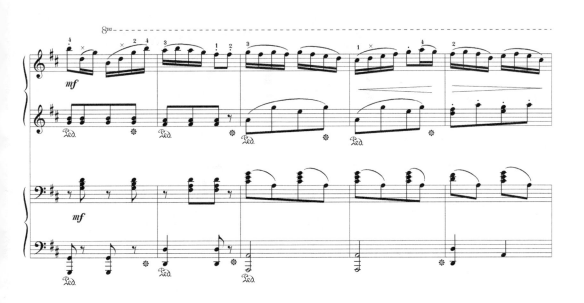

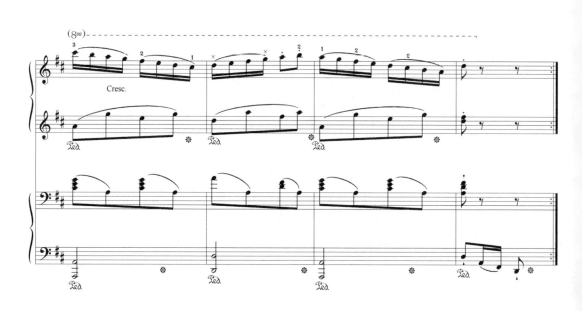

62. Jock O'Hazeldean

SIR WALTER SCOTT

Scots traditional
(arranger unknown)

"Why weep ye by the tide, la-dye? Why weep ye by the tide? I'll wed ye to my young-est son, And ye shall be his bride. And ye shall be his bride, la-dye, So come-ly to be seen," But aye she loot the tears down fa' For Jock O' Ha-zel-dean.

"Now let this wilfu' grief be done,
And dry that cheek so pale,
Young Frank is chief of Errington,
And Lord of Langley-dale.
His step is in the peaceful ha',
His sword in battle keen —"
But aye she loot the tears down fa',
for Jock O' Hazeldean.

"A chain o' gold ye shall not lack,
Nor braid to bind your hair,
Nor mettled hound, nor managed hawk,
Nor palfrey fresh and fair;
And you, the foremost o' them a',
Shall ride our forest queen —"
But aye she loot the tears down fa',
for Jock O' Hazeldean.

The kirk was deck'd at morning tide,
The taper glimmer'd fair,
The priest and bridegroom wait the bride,
And dame and knight are there.
They sought her baith by bower and ha',
The lady was not seen;
She's o'er the border, and awa
Wi' Jock O' Hazeldean.

63. My Boy Tammy

Hector MacNeil

Scottish

Moderato

Whar hae ye been a' day, my boy Tam - my? Whar hae ye been a' day, my boy Tam - my?

I've been by burn and flow' - ry brae, Mea - dow green and moun - tain gray, Court - ing o' this young thing,

just come frae her mam - my.

And whar gat ye that young thing, my boy Tammy?
And whar gat ye that young thing, my boy Tammy?
I gat her down in yonder how,
Smiling on a broomy know,
Herding a wee lamb and ewe for her poor mammy.

What said ye to the bonny bair, my boy Tammy?
What said ye to the bonny bair, my boy Tammy?
I praised her 'een, sae lovely blue,
Her dimpled cheek and cherry mou';
I pree'd it aft, as ye may trow--she said she'd tell her mammy.

I held her to my beating heart, my young, my smiling lammy!
I held her to my beating heart, my young, my smiling lammy!
I hae a house, it cost me dear,
I've walth op' plenishan and gear;
Ye's get it a' wer't ten times mair, gin ye will leave your mammy.

Has she been to kirk wi' thee, my boy Tammy?
Has she been to kirk wi' thee, my boy Tammy?
She has been to kirk wi' me,
And the tear was in her 'ee--
But oh! she's but a young thing, just come frae her mammy.

64. The Birks of Invermay

Scottish, setting by
PETER URBANI

vite   the   tune-ful   birds   to   sing, and   while they   war – ble

from   each   spray, Love   melts   the   u – ni   –   ver – sal   lay.

in soft rap - tures waste the day, A - mong the birks of

In - ver - may.

2

For soon the winter of the year,
And age, life's winter, will appear;
At this, thy living bloom will fade,
As that, will strip the verdant shade,
Our taste of pleasyre then is o'er
The feathered songsters are no more;
And when they droop, and we decay,
Adieu the birks of Invermay.

3

Behold the hills and vales around,
With lowing herds and flocks abound;
The wanton kids, and frisking lambs,
Gambol and dance about their dams;
The busy bees with humming noise,
And all the reptile kind rejoice:
Let us, like them, then sing and play
About the birks of Invermay.

4

Hark, how the waters, as they fall,
Loudly my love to gladness call;
The wanton waves sport in the beams,
And fishes play throughout the streams,
The circling sun does now advance,
And all the planets round him dance:
Let us as jovial be as they,
Among the birks of Invermay.

65. Good Night and Joy Be Wi' Ye

Alexander Boswell

arr. Franz Joseph Haydn

AN ANTHOLOGY OF MUSIC IN EARLY FLORIDA

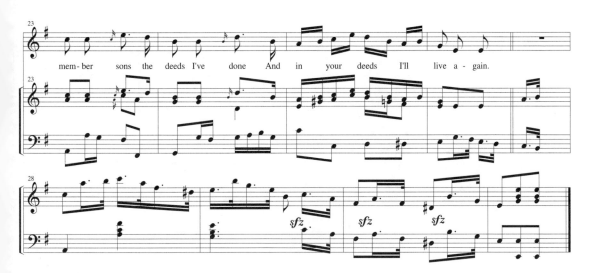

mem- ber   sons   the   deeds I've   done   And   in   your   deeds   I'll   live a - gain.

When on yon muir our gallant clan
Frae boasting foes their banners tore,
Wha shaw'd himself a better man,
Or fiercer wav'd the red claymore?
But when in peace, then mark me there
When thro' the glen the wandrer came,
I gave him of our hardy fare,
I gave him here a welcome hame.

The auld will speak, the young maun hear,
Be canty, but be good and leal;
Your ain ills ay he'e heart to bear.
Ainther's ay ha'e heart to feel
So, e'er I set, I'll see you shine,
I'll see you triumph e'er I fa';
My parting breath shall boast you mine;
Good night and joy be wi' ye a'!

muir - moor; claymore - two-edged sword; auld - old; maun - man;
leal - loyal, true; canty - cheerful, sprightly

66. Barbara Allan

"Twas at the hour"

Scottish
Arr. Franz Joseph Haydn

haste, and come to my mas-ter dear, Gin ye be Bar-b'ra Al-lan."

Vln.

D.S. al segno

O hooly, hooly gaed she up,
To the place where he was lying,
And when she drew the curtain by--
"Young man, I think you're dying!"
"O it's I'm sick, and very, very sick,
And 'tis a' for Barb'ra Allan!"
"O better for me ye's never be,
Tho' your heart's blood were a-spilling!"

And slowly, slowly raise she up,
And slowly, slowly left him,
And sighing, said, she could not stay,
Since death of life had reft him.
She had not gaen a mile but twa,
When she heard the dead-bell ringing,
And ev'ry jow that the dead-bell gied,
It cried, "Woe to Barb'ra Allan!"

"O dinna ye mind, young man," said she,
"When ye in the tavern was drinking,
That ye made the healths gae round and round,
And slighted Barb'ra Allan!"
He turn'd his face unto the wall,
And death was with him dealing--
"Adieu, Adieu, my dear friends all,
And be kind to Barb'ra Allan!"

"O mother, mother make my bed,
O make it soft and narrow;
Since my love died for me today,
I'll die for him tomorrow!"

67. The Exile of Erin

Savourneen Deelish

THOMAS MOORE

Old Irish Air,
arranged by
THOMAS CAMPBELL

1. There came to the reach a poor
3. "Oh! E - rin, my coun - try, the

Ex - ile of E - rin, The dew on his thin robe was hea - vy and chill, For his coun-try he sigh'd, when at
sad and for-sa - ken, In dreams I re - vis - it thy sea-beat-en shore; But, a - las! in a far for-eign

twi - light re - pair - ing, To wan - der a - lone by the wind - beat - en hill. But the
land I a - wak - en, And sigh for the friends who can meet me no more. Ah!

day - star at - tract - ed his eyes' sad de - vo - tion, For it rose o'er his own na - tive
cru - el fate! wilt thou ne - ver re - place me In a man - sion of peace, where no

isle of the o - cean, Where once in the fire of his youth - ful e - mo - tion, He
per - ils can chase me? Ah! ne - ver a - gain shall my bro - thers em - brace me! They

sang the bold an - them of E - rin go bragh. 2."Oh!
died to de - fend me, or live to de - plore! 4."Oh!

sad is my fate!" said the heart - bro - ken stran - ger, "The wild deer and wolf to a
where is my ca - bin door, fast by the wild wood? Sis - ters, and sire, did you

cov - ert can flee; But I have no ref - uge from fa - mine and dan - ger, A
weep for its fall? Oh! where is the moth - er that look'd on my child - hood? And

home and a coun - try re - main not to me; Ah! ne - ver a - gain in the
where is the bo - som friend, dear - er than all? Ah, my sad heart! long a -

green sha-dy bow-ers, Where my fore - fa-thers liv'd, shall I spend the sweet hours, Or
ban - don'd by pleas-ure, Why didst thou doat on a fast - fa-ding treas-ure? Tears

cov - er my harp with the wild-wo-ven flow-ers, And strike the sweet num - bers of
like the rain-drop may fall with-out meas - ure, But rap - ture and beau - ty they

E - rin go bragh.

5. "But

can - not re - call!

be thy fields, sweet-est isle of the o - cean, And thy harp - strik-ing bards sing a-

loud with de - vo - tion, Oh! E - rin, ma- vour - neen! E - rin go bragh!"

68. Roll the Cotton Down

Shanty - Arr. Stan Hugill

Oh 'a - way down south where I was born, Roll the cot-ton down! Oh! a - way down south a - round Cape Horn, We'll roll the cot - ton down! Roll the cot-ton, Roll the cot - ton Mos-es! Roll the cot- ton, oh! roll the cot - ton down!

Oh, away down south around Cape Horn,
Roll the cotton down!
Oh, we wisht to Christ we'd niver been born!
We'll roll the cotton down!
Full Chorus

We're bound away to Mobile Bay,
Roll the cotton down!
We're bound away at the break o'day,
We'll roll the cotton down!
Full Chorus

Oh, fare-ye-well we're bound to go,
Roll the cotton down!
Never let it be said we'll forget you,
We'll roll the cotton down!
Full Chorus

69. Clear the Track

Shanty - Arr. Stan Hugill

Oh, the smart-est clip-per you can find, Ah - hee, Ah - ho, are you most done, Is the

Marg - 'ret E- vans of the Black X Line, So clear a- way the track, let the Bull- gine run! To my

hey- rig- a- jig in a low- back car Ah - hee, ah- ho are you most done With Li- za Lee all on my knee, So

clear a- way the track, let the Bull- gine run!

70. John, Come Tell Us as We Haul Away

Mobile Bay

Shanty - Arr. Stan Hugill

Not too fast

From Liv - er- pool town we sailed a- way, John, come tell us as we haul a-way! Out - ward bound at the

break of day. John, come tell us as we haul a-way! Aye, aye, haul, aye, John, come tell us as we haul a-way!

First Shantyman:
Wuz ye never down in Mobile Bay?
John, come tell us as we haul away!
A-screwin' cotton all the day?
John, come tell us as we haul away!
Aye, aye, haul, aye,
John, come tell us as we haul away!

Second Shantyman:
Oh, yes, I've bin down Mobile Bay,
So he tells us as we haul away!
A-screwin' cotton all the day,
So he tells us as we haul away!
Aye, aye, haul, aye,
So he tells us as we haul away!

First Shantyman:
An' what did yer do in Mobile Bay?
Did you give that flash tart all yer pay?

Second Shantyman:
Oh, this I did in Mobile Bay,
I courted this gal who's name was May.

Second Shantyman:
I married her in Mobile Bay,
An' lived there happy many a day.

71. Sir Roger de Coverley

Cavalier and Lady.

arranged by
MARI RUEF HOFER

72. The Forked Deer

Scottish - arr. R.P. Christeson

73. Fisher's Hornpipe

Fiddle Tune, arranged by
R. P. CHRISTESON

74. Leather Breeches

Fiddle Tune, arranged by
R. P. CHRISTESON

75a. Green Gravel

Somerset

Arr. Cecil J. Sharp

Green gra-vel, green gra-vel, the grass is so green, The fair-est young la-dy that ev-er was seen; O

Ma-ry, O Ma-ry, your true love is dead, We send you a let-ter to turn 'round your head. I wash you in

D.C. ad lib

milk! I dress you in silk, I write down your name with a gold pen and ink.

"The players form a ring with joined hands and dance round slowly...At the end of the fourth line the child named (*Mary* in the text) looses hands, turns round and rejoins the ring facing outward, i.e., with back to the center. The stanza is repeated until, one by one, each player has turned round in the way just described. In some versions, the process is then reversed, the players, on being named, successively turning their faces to the center of the ring."

75b. Green Gravel

Florida African-American Children Version

English

Green grav-el, green grav-el, The grass is so green, The fair-est of maid-ens That e-ver was seen.

Miss Mary, Miss Mary,	Green gravel, green gravel,	Miss Mary, Miss Mary,
Your sweetheart is dead;	The grass is so green,	Your true love's not slain;
The king sends you a letter,	All over creation,	The king sends you a letter,
So turn back your head.	A shame to be seen.	So turn round again.

"The players form a circle and march round hand in hand as they sing. When Miss Mary is addressed, she turns her head round to the right and marches backward. As the first stanza is repeated, the person to the right becomes Miss Mary, and so on until all in the circle are marching one way and looking the other. Then the second stanza is sung, and all players turn heads to the left and repeat the game if desired."

76. Shule Agra

Irish traditional,
arranged by
MARGARET BONI
& NORMAN LLOYD

Shule agra = Come, my love

Go thee, thu Mavourneen slaun = Farewell, my darling

3.

I'll dye my petticoat, I'll dye it red,
And round the world I'll beg my bread,
Till I find my love alive or dead.
Go thee, thu Mavourneen slaun.
Chorus

4.

King James was routed in the fray;
The "wild-geese" went with him away,
My boy went too, that dreary day.
Go thee, thu Mavourneen slaun.
Chorus

77. Robin Adair

Caroline Keppel

Andante con moto

Gaelic

Arr. Norman Lloyd

What's this dull town to me? Ro-bin's not near. What was't I wish'd to see, What wish'd to hear?

Where's all the joy and mirth Made this town a heav'n on earth? Oh, they are all fled with thee, Ro-bin A - dair.

What made th'assembly shine? Robin Adair.
What made the ball so fine? Robin was there.
What when the play was o'er, What made my heart so sore?
Oh, it was the parting with Robin Adair.

But now thou'rt cold to me, Robin Adair,
But now thou'rt cold to me, Robin Adair,
Yet he I lov'd so well, Still in my heart shall dwell.
Oh, I can ne'er forget, Robin Adair.

78. The Girl I Left Behind Me

arranged by
J. C. VIERECK

The hour was sad I left the maid, A ling'-ring fare-well tak - ing, Her sighs and tears my steps de-lay'd, I thought her heart was break - ing, In hur-ried words her name I bless'd, I breath'd the vows that bind me, And

nas - sas plain, Where in the post as - sign'd me, I shar'd the glo - ry

of that fight, Sweet girl I left be - hind me. Full
The

ma - ny a name our ban - ners bore, Of for - mer deeds of dar - ing, But
hope of fi - nal vic - to - ry With - in my bo - som burn - ing, Is

they were of the days of yore, In which we had no shar - ing; But
ming - ling with sweet thoughts of thee, And of my fond re - turn - ing; But

now, our lau - rels fresh - ly won, With the old ones shall en - twin'd be, Still wor - thy of our
should I ne'er re - turn a - gain, Still worth thy love thou'lt find me, Dis - hon - or's breath shall

sires each son, Sweet girl I left be - hind me.
nev - er stain The name I leave be - hind me.

Chapter 8

The Social Circle

Florida began to appear in titles of music in the nineteenth century. Tunes titled "Florida" were written for collections of sacred music. The earliest was by Truman S. Wentmore in *Mercer's Cluster,* an 1854 collection favored by the Baptists. Dance music was favored by St. Augustine musicians, including "Florida Schottisch" (No. 79) by G. Torrente and a "Florida" waltz (No. 80) by Theo. von la Hache. Only the trio of the waltz has survived in a St. Augustine collection. Both pieces are well crafted.

Orchestras and theatrical companies were welcomed by the French population of Pensacola in the early 1820s. Solomon Smith managed the nearby Mobile opera company, and French opera prospered in New Orleans. Prince Achille Murat and other affluent Florida residents visited New York and the cultural centers of Europe, but their small communities could not support productions of large-scale musical events. They did have local pianists and singers who were well supplied with standard and current compositions. Pianists acquired libraries of fantasies, variations on folk tunes, sentimental songs, and operas. Overtures and arias from operas became parlor pieces for piano. One bound collection included the overture to *Il Tancredi* (No. 81), which Rossini composed before his twenty-first birthday. Few Floridians had heard the opera, but their emotions were undoubtedly engaged by the Italianate melodies.

Preachers denounced the waltz as sinful when it was introduced in America. Florida's Prince Achille Murat observed the uproar when he attended first performances of that dance in New York. American audiences had yet to appreciate the artistry of famous dancers Marie Taglioni, Cerito, and Fanny Elssler. Cosmopolitan Murat and certain affluent Florida families had seen these stage performers abroad or on their American tours. Dancers became well known in Florida largely because pianists played sheet music of their dances. Among them were Taglioni's "La Trènis" from *La Sylphide* (No. 82), Fanny Elssler's "La Cachucka," the "Cracovienne," and the Quadrilles from Auber's opera *Le Dieu et la Bayadère* (Nos. 83a, 83b, and 83c), as danced by Mademoiselle Augusta and published in New York by Hewitt and Jacques.

As early as the late 1820s, theatrical dancing was often incorporated into dramas and operas by professional companies in Pensacola. A Mrs. Hartwig was a favored dancer. She offered lessons to individuals or groups while the drama group was in town.

Skill in social dancing in the first half of the nineteenth century may be attributed to the care of the dancing masters. A Mr. Suter from Charleston offered instruction and arranged cotillion parties in St. Augustine in 1823. In Tallahassee in the 1830s, a Mr. Tarteen taught the traditional Spanish Dance, along with lancers, quadrilles, Caledonias, mazurkas, the gallopade, the polka, and the then-daring waltz. In Pensacola both French and Spanish residents danced ceremonial marches for dramatic entrances and promenades. They danced the up-tempo fandango, probably accompanied by guitar and castanets. Their great passion of the season, however, was the formal Carnival masquerade. Colorfully costumed dancers, not always with refinement but with spirit and enjoyment, disported the skills they acquired under their socially correct tutors. A sophisticated young army officer once commented that the spectacle exceeded his most sanguine expectations.

As social evenings wore on, Floridians danced country dances, just as their English and Scottish counterparts did. Strathspeys and reels were popular, as were hornpipes and other tunes played by fiddlers. Many of them are known to line dancers even today.

The popularity of dancing in Florida during the Spanish and British periods has been noted earlier in this book. Minuets and country dances of England and Scotland were known by British military men and their partners. In St. Augustine, Minorcans and later Spanish settlers continued the tradition of slow, graceful Spanish dances. By the beginning of statehood days, the dances were augmented to include square-shaped quadrilles and cotillions, round-shaped polonaises and waltzes, and the running glissade. The waltz, not then accepted in northern states, became the favored dance in both Pensacola and Tallahassee in the second and third decades of the nineteenth century.

Expanding the role of dancing master in the 1850s was a Mr. Rasimi, who had studied his art in the academies of London and Paris. He scheduled classes for Tallahassee women and children in daytime hours and for men in the evening. Two of his students were daughters of Governor Thomas Brown. Local pianists abetted the dancing rage by learning to play strathspeys, gallops, marches, polkas, schottisches, and mazurkas. At week-end parties, dances were well regulated and programmed to accommodate a variety of tempos and partners.

Three dances popular across the nation in the 1840s were in the repertory of St. Augustine pianists and dancers. "Katy-Did Polka" (No. 84) was composed by the famous showman Louis Antoine Jullien; "Cally Polka" (No. 85) was arranged by Allen Dodworth as performed by the excellent Dodworth Band; and "The Hope Waltzes" (No. 86) included one waltz by B. Hope and the "Wilde Rosen Waltz" (1847) by Johann Strauss the younger (1825–1899). These pieces were also played by Florida Confederate bands.

Thomas Dartmouth Rice was introduced in 1829 to Pensacola audiences as a comic and dancer in *The Cobbler's Daughter, or, Old Hucks Outwitted*. Three years later he arrived in New York and took the city by storm. In the years between, he served his apprenticeship in numerous roles with traveling drama companies. His greatest success came from singing and dancing "Jim Crow" (No. 87) in blackface minstrel shows. He fashioned his act after a black street performance. His wheeling, swaying, and jumping coordinated with outrageous gestures and with the lyrics of the song. Exaggeration and comic brags filled every verse. In the song he was a fiddler rivaling Paganini, an irresistible lover, a big-game hunter, and a compelling speaker in the U.S. House of Representatives. Rice became an international star, based largely on his lively presentation of his sympathetic, happy blackface character.

Queen Victoria conferred a knighthood on Henry Rowles Bishop in 1842. The public had awarded him their favor nineteen years earlier, when his composition "Home, Sweet Home" (No. 88) was first performed. They and subsequent generations made it the most popular song of the English-speaking world in the nineteenth century. It was sung by such luminaries as Jenny Lind, Adelina Patti, and Maria Malibran as well as by Florida parlor singers. Pianists played variations on it, and soldiers in opposing armies of the Civil War sang it from cheap songbooks. It was a simple melody, with a range of only an octave and a harmonic language of the three basic chords. The sentimental words of John Howard Payne had universal appeal to all who were world-weary and longing for a haven. It mattered not if that haven was a "lowly thatch'd cottage" or heaven itself.

For the agile coloraturas of the nineteenth century, Henry R. Bishop wrote his famous "Echo Song" (No. 89). It had a two-octave spread and called for vocal trickery only the best singers could negotiate satisfactorily. Nonetheless, it was attempted by Florida vocalists and continued to be performed where an equally agile flutist was available to alternate the echoes.

The English composer Charles Edward Horn came to New York in 1827 and became active in the musical life of the city. He adapted operas of other composers, wrote five of his own, held musical soirées, wrote an oratorio, and owned a music publishing business. He is not remembered today for his large-scale works but for his songs. "Cherry Ripe," one of his best, was sung by a children's choir at the old Pisgah church near Tallahassee in 1854. Parlor singers in Florida sang "Near the Lake Where Drooped the Willow" (No. 90), which was published in 1839 by Hewitt and Jacques as a "Southern Refrain." The tune was arranged by Horn with words by the eminent writer George P. Morris. The eminent American music historian Gilbert Chase has written that the tune was an old African-American melody arranged as a comic minstrel song. Adapted to a "refined text," it appeared in a religious version in the first edition of William Walker's *Southern Harmony.*

"Hope Told a Flatt'ring Tale" (No. 91) by Giovanni Paisiello is a plaint from a disappointed lover. It is an "ironed-out" version of "Nel cor più non mi sento" encased in the usual *da capo* formula, the first section in major, the second in minor. Paisiello wrote operas for Napoleon I, Catherine the Great, and Ferdinand IV. He also wrote them for Joseph Bonaparte and for Joachim Murat, King of Naples, who was the father of Achille Murat. The young Achille Murat moved to St. Augustine in 1824 and a year later relocated to Tallahassee, where he spent his later years. This song was bound in an 1836 sheet-music collection from an East Florida family. It was published in Charleston by J. Sieling (1819–25), as well as in New York and Philadelphia.

The text to "The Harper's Song" (No. 92) appeared in the 1830s Tallahassee newspapers just as it did in those of New York. The song was typical of those sung by Wirt family members in Jefferson County. It is in a bound collection of that family's papers in the University of West Florida Library. B. F. Peale arranged the Spanish guitar accompaniment. The original version for solo voice and piano accompaniment by T. V. Wiesenthal was published in Philadelphia by G. Willig. The words are from "Rokeby" by Sir Walter Scott.

Jenny Lind was the singing idol of Floridians in the 1840s just as she was of other Americans. Her tours, arranged by P. T. Barnum and accompanied by the great showman's advertising campaign and favorable reviews, assured her fame. Arrangers and publishers brought out editions of many of her songs. "My Home, My Happy Home" (No. 93) was one of the most popular songs in Florida at the time.

Among the German art songs sung in Pensacola in the first half of the eighteenth century were Schubert's "Serenade," Abt's "Schlaf wohl, du süsser Engel du!" (No. 94), and Franz's "Er ist gekommen" ("His Coming"; No. 95). Each of the three sections of the latter is composed of two rising melodies made appealing by altered chords in the accompaniments and alternations between major and minor modes.

Stephen Foster's early songs were in the tradition of those written by such British composers as Bishop and Linley. They were sentimental or nostalgic, suited to home or stage performance, and only a few show a slight influence of either Italian opera arias or German *lieder*. About thirty were written for performance by E. P. Christy's Minstrels or other groups. Usually the verses were for solo and the choruses for ensemble. They were strophic, with simple accompaniments. Many were in dialect set to banjo effects and were followed by a closing section that was to be danced.

Several Middle Florida families have left bound sheet-music collections that included Foster's songs and piano elaborations of the tunes. Included here are "Camptown Races" (No. 96) and "Nelly Bly" (No. 97), both popular minstrel songs, and "Beautiful Dreamer" (No. 98), a solo serenade.

The song "Zip Coon" (No. 99) was sung by an African-American dandy who wore a long-tailed blue coat. He was created in the text by either Bob Farnell or G. W. Dixon—both claimed authorship. The seven verses touch on such subjects as courting, politics, and death, but the stories are so outrageous and the choruses so nonsensical that the minstrel audiences could only have been amused. Floridians from Pensacola to Key West sang this minstrel song. Fiddlers played it, calling it "Turkey in the Straw." It was popularized by the blackface singing comic George Washington Dixon beginning in the late 1820s. It may be heard today as a country dance fiddle tune.

"Wood Up Quick Step" (No. 100) was a spirited tune played by Florida bands. It was also played on the piano by Susan Branch, niece of Governor John Branch, and on the guitar by Julia A. Cole in Pensacola. The guitar edition was published in Philadelphia by G. E. Blake. In Florida, the title referred to taking on of fuel by steamboats. A piano edition by J. Holloway was published in Philadelphia by A. Fiot.

Many settlers who moved to Florida in the nineteenth century called it paradise, but like immigrants to other territories and states, they sang of their longing for home. Soldiers and sailors stationed at the numerous military posts sang these same songs. They were transient residents, but when their assignments were over, many chose to live out their remaining years in their earthly paradise. Heaven could wait.

One of the homesickness songs heard most frequently was a German tune titled the "Switzer's Song of Home" (No. 101). Washington Ives, a Confederate soldier from Live Oak, once wrote that his sister played this tune on her piano. Ives was a member of the Fourth Florida Regiment band when they played it in September 1863 at a camp near Chattanooga, Tennessee.

Music was employed to help raise funds to support almost every cause that good churchmen and respectable citizens regarded as worthy. The Tallahassee Ladies Memorial Association held a festival and fair in December 1866 to raise money for a suitable monument to the Confederate dead. Music was furnished by the Seventh Infantry Band. The band also played for a dance that raised a sizeable amount of money, although local ministers declared dancing a sin. Minstrel shows were used to raise money for the eradication of ringworm, and salubrity societies sang songs of temperance to church members and town drunks. Circuses, with their bands and theatrical companies, came to town. Ministers warned that circus performers had loose morals and that the money they took from citizens would be better used in support of local charities. Some socially prominent church members, however, attended the performances, risking a little damage to their souls. "Nothing Else To Do" (No. 102) was heard as a comic circus act or an intermission song at a theatrical performance. Though it is a man's narrative, Miss Rosina Shaw and many Florida ladies sang it to unbounded applause. According to George P. Reed, the Boston publisher, the words to the song were compiled from an old American ballad. The copyright date is 1839. "Nothing Else To Do" is an amusing biographical sketch of a young man who went a-courting. Five verses later, he is the father of "a healthy rosy set of lads and lassies." He loves "the little rogues that caus'd us something else to do."

79. Florida Schottish

Andante un poco animato

G. Torrente

80. Florida

Theo. von la Hache

81. Overture from *Il Tancredi*

Gioacchino Rossini.

6

82. La Trènis, from *La Sylphide*

Jean Schneitzhoffer

Forward two - Cross over - Chassé - Cross to places - Balancé and turn partner - Ladies chain - Promenade half round and half right and left to places.

83a. L'Eté, from *Le Dieu et la Bayadère*

D.F.E. Auber

Figure 1. Forward two, cross over, to the right and to the left, Cross over 2. Balancès.

83b. La Pantalon, from *Le Dieu et la Bayadère*

D.F.E. Auber

Figure 1. Right and left. 2. Balancès.
3. Ladies chain. 4. Half promenade.

83c. Brahma, from *Le Dieu et la Bayadère*

D.F.E. Auber

Figure 1. Ladies chain 2. Forward two, cross over, to the right and to the left, cross over 3. Side four to the right 4. Balancès all 5. Chassez eight

84. Katy-Did Polka

or Souvenirs of Castle Garden

LOUIS ANTOINE JULLIEN.

85. Cally Polka

As performed by DODWORTH'S BAND.

Arranged by ALLEN DODWORTH.

AN ANTHOLOGY OF MUSIC IN EARLY FLORIDA

2

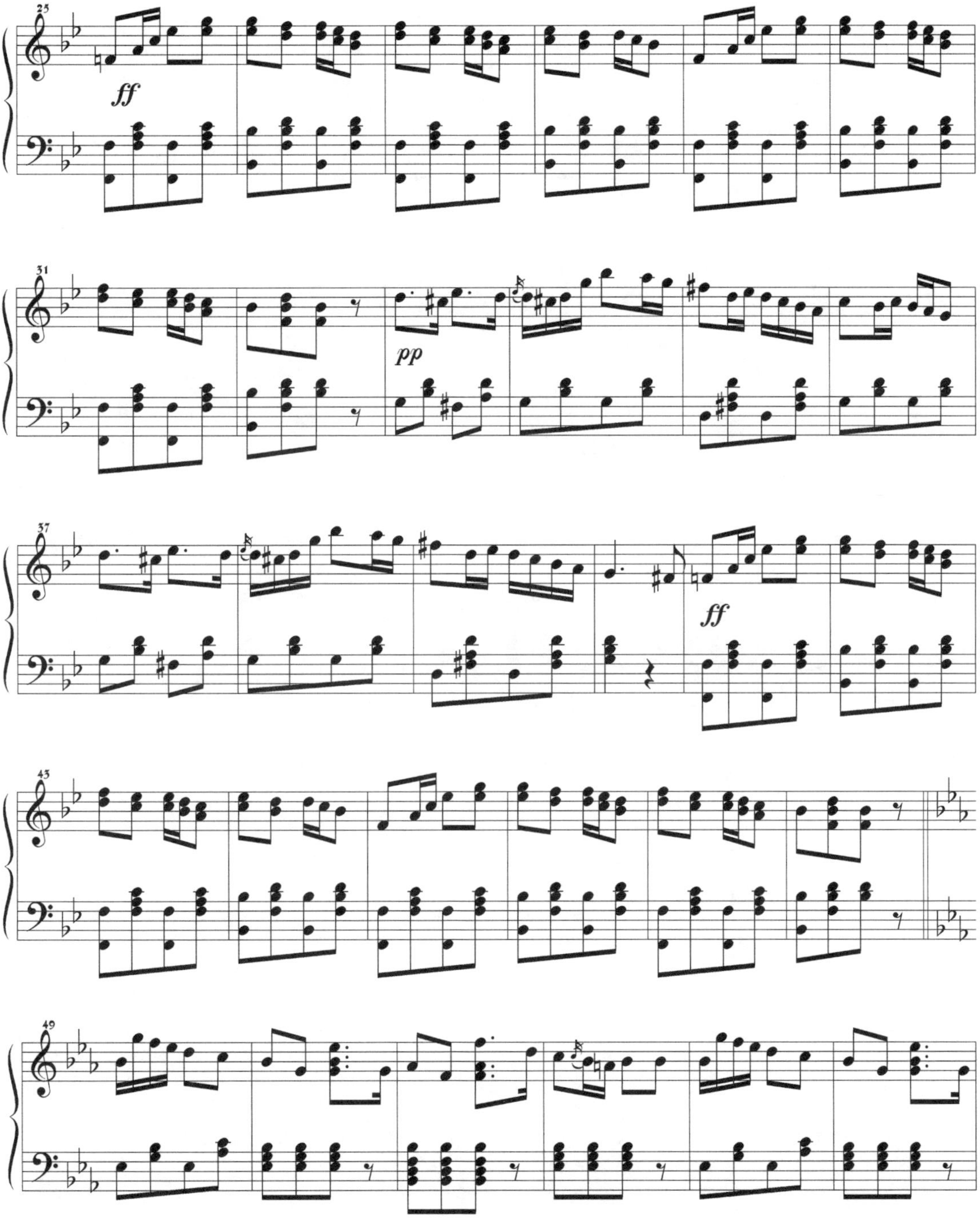

86. The Hope Waltzes

B. Hope

87. Jim Crow

Allegretto

T.D. Rice

Come lis-ten all you gals and boys, I'm just from Tuck-y hoe; I'm goin to sing a lee-tle song, My name's Jim Crow. Weel a-bout, and turn a-bout, And do jis so; Eb'-ry time I weel a-bout, I jump Jim Crow.

I'm a rorer on de fiddle,
An down in ole Virginny;
Dey say I play de skientific,
Like massa Pagganinny.

I met Miss Dina Scrub one day,
I gib her sich a buss,
An den she turn an slap my face,
An make a mighty fuss.

I wip de lion ob de west,
I eat de Allegator;
I put more water in my mouf,
Den boil ten load ob tater.

De way de bake de hoe cake,
Virginny nebber tire,
De put de doe upon de foot,
An stick im in de fire.

I take de walk to Niblows,
'Wid Dina by my side;
An dare we see Miss Watson,
De Paganini bride.

She sing so lubly dat my heart,
Went pit a pat jis so;
I wish she fall in lub wid me,
I'd let Miss Dina go.

88. Home, Sweet Home

John Howard Payne

Henry R. Bishop

Chorus

Home, home, sweet, sweet home! There's no place like home, there's no place like home.

An exile from home, splendour dazzles in vain:
Oh! give me my lowly thatch'd cottage again;
The birds singing gaily, that come at my call;
Give me them with that peace of mind, dearer than all.
Home! home! sweet, sweet home;
There's no place like home, there's no place like home!

How sweet 'tis to sit 'neath a fond father's smile,
And the cares of a mother to soothe and beguile;
Let others delight 'mid new pleasures to roam,
But give me, oh! give me the pleasures of home.
Home! home! sweet, sweet home;
But give me, oh give me the pleasures of home.

To thee I'll return, overburden'd with care,
The heart's dearest solace will smile on me there;
No more from that cottage again will I roam,
Be it ever so humble, there's no place like home.
Home! home! sweet, sweet home;
There's no place like home, there's no place like home.

89. Echo Song

SIR HENRY R. BISHOP.

2

way, and steal my soul a - way, and steal my soul a - way, And

steal my soul a - way. Still, still I hear the

change - ful strain. It mocks, it e - choes, it

it e-choes a - gain!

90. Near the Lake Where Drooped the Willow

GEORGE P. MORRIS.

CHARLES E. HORN.

Long time a - go!

2.

Rock, and tree, and flowing water, Long time ago!
Bird, and bee, and blossom taught her, Love's spell to know!
While to my fond words she listened, Murmuring low,
Tenderly her dove eyes glistened, Long time ago!

3.

Mingled were our hearts forever! Long time ago!
Can I now forget her? never! No, lost one, no!
To her grave these tears are given, Ever to flow!
She's the star I missed from heaven; Long time ago!

91. Hope Told a Flatt'ring Tale

Giovanni Paisiello

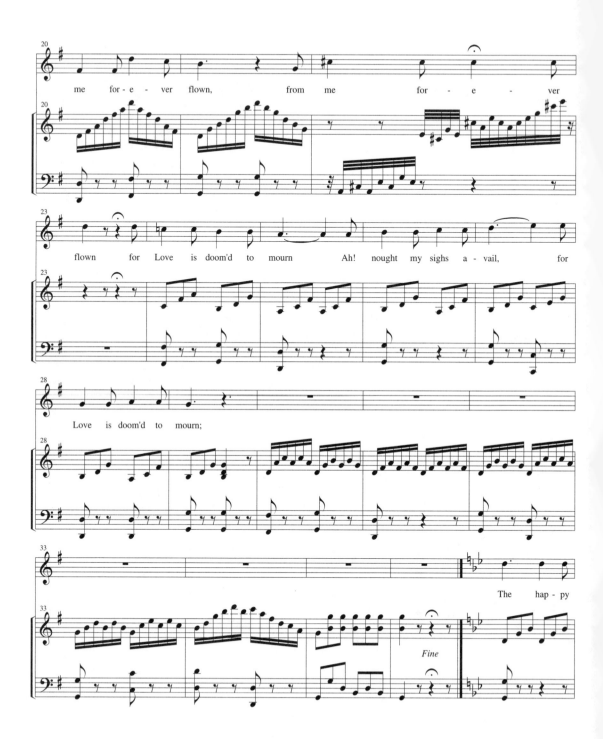

dream of love is o'er, and Life a - las! can charm no

more, the hap - py dream of love is o'er, Life a -

las! can charm no more, can charm no more.

92. The Harper's Song

SIR WALTER SCOTT.

T.V. WIESENTHAL.

AN ANTHOLOGY OF MUSIC IN EARLY FLORIDA

in;   Oh take him   in;   Take   the wan - d'ring

Har - per in;   Take   the wan - d'ring Har - per in.

2.
Bid not me, in battle field,
Buckler lift, or broad sword wield;
All my strength and all my art
Is to touch the gentle heart,
With the wizard notes that ring
From the peaceful minstrel string.
     (The minstrel string.)

3.
I have song of war for knight,
Lay of love for lady bright,
Fairy tale to lull the ear,
Goblin grim the maids to scare;
Dark the night, and long till day
Do not bid me farther stray;
     (Not farther stray;)

93. My Home, My Happy Home

G. A. HODSON.

My home, my home, my hap - py home, spot

I've jour - ney'd from thee, far and near, But

94. Schlaf wohl, du süsser Engel du!

du!
pose.

Schlaf' wohl, du
Sleep well, dear

lie - ber sü - sser En - gel du!
an - gel, sweet be thy re - pose.

pp

95. Er ist gekommen

FRIEDRICH RÜCKERT
Translated by John S. Dwight

ROBERT FRANZ
OPUS 4, NO. 7

ALLEGRO AGITATO.

Er ist ge - kom - men in Sturm und Re - gen,
Wild was the day when he came with greet - ing;

ihm schlug be - klom - men mein Herz ent - ge - ben.
For him how wild - ly my heart was beat - ing.

Wie konnt' ich ah - nen, dass sei - ne Bah - nen sich
Could I be know - ing That he was go - ing Up -

PIANO.

con Ped.

er   auf al   -   len, al   -   len   We - gen.

mine   still tru   -   ly, tru   -   ly   beat - ing.

96. Camptown Races

STEPHEN COLLINS FOSTER.

day!   I'll bet my money on de bob - tail nag,   Some - bo-dy bet on de

bay.

2.
De long tail fly and de big black hoss — Doo-dah! doo-dah!
Dey fly de track and dey both cut across — Oh! doo-dah day!
De blind hoss sticken in a big mud hole — Doo-dah! doo-dah!
Can't touch bottom wid a ten foot pole — Oh! doo-dah day!
     CHORUS.

3.
Old muley cow come on to de track — Doo-dah! doo-dah!
De bob-tail fling her ober his back — Oh! doo-dah day!
Den fly along like a rail-road car — Doo-dah! doo-dah!
Runnin' a race wid a shootin' star — Oh! doo-dah day!
     CHORUS.

4.
See dem flyin' on a ten mile heat — Doo-dah! doo-dah!
Round de race-track, den repeat — Oh! doo-dah day!
I win my money on de bob-tail nag — Doo-dah! doo-dah!
I keep my money in an old tow-bag — Oh! doo-dah day!
     CHORUS.

97. Nelly Bly

STEPHEN COLLINS FOSTER.

Nel-ly Bly! Nel-ly Bly! bring de broom a-long, We'll sweep de kit-chen clean, my dear, and hab a lit-tle song.

Poke de wood, my la-dy lub, And make de fire burn, And while I take de ban-jo down, Just gib de mush a turn.

CHORUS.

Heigh! Nel - ly Ho! Nel - ly, lis - ten lub to me, I'll sing for you play for you, a dul - cem mel - o - dy.

Heigh! Nel - ly Ho! Nel - ly, lis - ten lub to me, I'll sing for you play for you, a dul - cem mel - o - dy.

Heigh! Nel - ly Ho! Nel - ly, lis - ten lub to me, I'll sing for you play for you, a dul - cem mel - o - dy.

Heigh! Nel - ly Ho! Nel - ly, lis - ten lub to me, I'll sing for you play for you, a dul - cem mel - o - dy.

2d Verse. Nel-ly Bly hab a voice like de tur-tle-dove, I hears it in de mea-dow and I hears it in de grove.

Nel-ly Bly hab a heart warm as cup ob tea, And big-ger dan de sweet po-ta-to down in Ten-nes-see.

Chorus.

3rd Verse. Nel-ly Bly shuts her eye when she goes to sleep, When she wa-kens up a-gain her eye-balls gin to peep. De

way she walks, she lifts her foot, and den she brings it down, And when it lights der's mu-sic dah in dat part ob de town.

Chorus.

4th Verse. Nel-ly Bly! Nel-ly Bly! neb-ber, neb-ber sigh, Neb-ber bring de tear drop to de cor-ner ob your eye, For de

pie is made ob pun-kins and de mush is made ob corn, And der's corn and pun-kins plen-ty lub a-ly-in in de barn.

Chorus.

98. Beautiful Dreamer

STEPHEN COLLINS FOSTER.

List while I woo thee with soft mel - o - dy;
E'en as the morn on the stream - let and sea;
Gone are the cares of
Then will all clouds of

life's bu - sy throng,
sor - row de - part,
Beau - ti - ful dream - er, a - wake un - to me!
Beau - ti - ful dream - er, a - wake un - to me!

Beau - ti - ful dreamer, a - wake un - to me!
Beau - ti - ful dreamer, a - wake un - to me!

Ad Lib.

A Tempo.

99. Zip Coon

G.W. Dixon

Allegro maestoso

O ole Zip Coon he is a larn-ed sko-ler, O

ole Zip Coon he is a larn-ed sko-lar O ole Zip Coon he is a larn-ed sko-lar Sings

pos-sum up a gum tree an coo-ny in a hol-ler. Pos-sum up a gum tree, coo-ny on a stump,

I went down to Sandy hollar t'other afternoon
And the first man I chanced to meet war ole Zip Coon;
Ole Zip Coon he is a natty scholar,
For he plays upon de Banjo "Cooney in de hollar."

I pose you heard ob de battle New Orleans,
Whar ole Gineral Jackson gib de British beans;
Dare ye Yankee boys do de job so slick,
For dey cotch ole Packenham an rowed him up de creek.

I hab so many tings to tork about, but I don't know which come first,
So here de toast to old Zip Coon before he gin to rust;
May he hab de pretty girls, like de King ob ole,
To sing dis song so many times, 'fore he turn to mole.

100. Wood Up Quick Step

JOHN HOLLOWAY BLANCHOR.

101. Switzer's Song of Home

I. Moscheles

All that's dear to me is wanting,
Lone and cheerless hear I roam;
The stranger's joy's howe'er enchanting;
To me can never be like Home,
To me can never be like Home.

Was mir fehit mir Alles,
Bin so ganz verlassen hier,
Ist's auch schon im fremden Lande,
Dennoch wird's zur Heimath nie,
Dennoch wird's zur Heimath nie.

Give me those, I ask no other,
Those that bless the humble dome,
Where dwell my Father and my Mother,
Give, Oh! give me back my home,
My own, my own dear native Home.

In die Heimath mocht ich wieder,
Lieber aber lieber bald,
Mocht zum Vater, mocht zur Mutter,
Mocht zu Berg zu Thal und Wald,
Mocht zu Berg zu Thal und Wald.

102. Nothing Else To Do

Herbert Fry

J.L. Hatton

Arr. W. A. Newland

'Twas down in yond valley together we sat,
And passed away the hours in curious chat,
I told her I lov'd her, I hop'd she lov'd me too,
So we'd love one another for we'd nothing else to do...

She hung down her head and with blushes replied,
I lov'd you from the first, you must make me your bride,
Without hesitation I made her this vow,
I'll marry you my dear for I've nothing else to do...

So to the next village away we did roam,
In search of a clergy we found him at home,
I paid him his fee he made one of us two,
And married us straight way for he'd nothing else to do...

We liv'd in felicity in joy and content,
And never knew the sorrows of those that do repent
Our neighbors around us were loyal and true,
And we lov'd one another for we'd nothing else to do...

The change which years have brought I should tell you in this place
Our table is too small and our cottage wanting space
We've a healthy rosy set of lads and lassies too
And we love the little rogues that caus'd us something else to do...

Chapter 9

The Men in Gray and the Folks at Home

Several sentimental songs remained favorites in Florida for many years in the nineteenth century. At a forecastle concert aboard the *Albatross* during the Seminole Wars, "Alice Gray" (No. 103) and "Oft in the Stilly Night" (No. 104) survived inept performances, and both continued to be popular with Florida soldiers during the Confederacy. Henry Russell's "Cheer! Boys, Cheer!" (No. 105) continued to spark optimism among Florida boys who had sung it years before their enlistment. The song is a farewell to England, as men board a ship sailing westward, where wealth and good fortune await. "Kathleen Mavourneen" (No. 106), written by P. N. Crouch, a Confederate bugler in the Richmond Howitzers, is the story of a sad Irish romance. This edition, published in Columbia, South Carolina, was especially popular as a song of farewell among Confederate troops, including those from Florida.

Stephen Foster wrote parlor songs, "Ethiopian" tunes, and plantation songs. "Old Folks at Home" (No. 107) was his most famous. It was published by in New York by Firth, Pond and Company in 1851 under the name E. P. Christy, but later Foster claimed it as his own. Unlike many minstrel songs, it did not depict slaves as congenitally happy, but tapped the deeply sentimental feelings of one who had been separated from his family. The sad and lonely singer remembered the days of his youth. He longed to return to the plantation, to live and die with his family. He wondered when he again would hear the banjo "tumming." The piece was probably chosen as Florida's state song because of the appeal of its pathetic theme, its tender sentiment toward the singer's Suwannee homeland, and its universal popularity. The theme, as musicologist William W. Austin points out, is not far removed from that of the Irish patriots or Swiss mountaineers who sang about their own homelands. Austin also suggests that the singer might have been a slave of the Seminole nation before being removed to the West. He bases this conjecture on General Thomas Sidney Jesup's insistence that the 1835–42 Seminole Wars were "Negro wars" rather than "Indian wars." He also affirms that both Native Americans and slaves were runaways and both were called Seminoles. He quotes a passage by Br. Captain John T. Sprague, U.S. Eighth Infantry, declaring the Seminole's "love of home."

In minstrel shows, white men in blackface cracked jokes about local prominent people, improvised unconventional impersonation dances, and sang plaintive, sentimental songs. Profound ideas were embedded deeply in humor. In "Old Folks at Home," the theme is love of home, but this time the music setting is upbeat. The singer has wandered to Kentucky but longs to return home. The song has a unison chorus rather than the usual mixed-voice setting.

Several of Foster's songs are contained in bound volumes of sheet music compiled by early Floridians. The lyric serenade "Come Where My Love Lies Dreaming" (No. 108) is among them. One edition was scored for solo voice and another for four voices. The latter was chosen for this anthology. Unlike the usual solo verses and quartet chorus, this work is for mixed quartet throughout. The melody is one of Foster's best. At two junctures, the three lower voices assume an accompanying function in the manner of plucked strings. An eight-measure transposition to the dominant key supplies variety before a final return to the original. Foster's extraordinary gift for melody is matched by appealing lyrics. In addition, the sentiment matched perfectly the taste of nineteenth-century America.

Like many in similar situations, Richard Milburn, a black messenger boy from Philadelphia, augmented his income by giving street performances in return for the loose change of passersby. He would play the guitar and whistle a catchy tune that imitated a mockingbird. Septimus Winner, a Philadelphia songwriter, assured the melody of immortality in American popular music history by setting it to a sentimental verse and a rhythmically appealing chorus that he titled "Listen to the Mocking Bird" (No. 109). Listening to the tune only, one would hardly suspect that the verse might be a melancholy reminiscence of a September love. The tune has the bounce of a minstrel tune, yet the anomaly of sad words and happy tune did not dent the tune's popularity for many generations. It was published in 1855, and both Confederate and Union soldiers sang it. Florida pianists played "The Mocking Bird Quick Step," arranged by J. A. Rosenberger and published in Richmond in 1864. Winner used many pseudonyms, and issued this song under the name of Alice Hawthorne.

The original "Wait for the Wagon" (No. 110) was a lively courting song sung by a farmer to his sweetheart. It was written by R. P. Buckley and sung by his Serenaders, a minstrel troupe. The tune and chorus were picked up by both Republicans and Democrats during the campaign for the presidency in 1856. New texts were devised for the campaign between Lincoln and McClellan in 1864. As the Civil War became a reality, parodies appeared both in favor of the Union and of secession. Florida boys sang "The Southern Wagon," which named the first seven states of the Confederacy—Florida was one of them. An early Pensacola collection of sheet music includes an edition with a guitar accompaniment.

"Dixie's Land" (No. 111), written by Daniel Emmett for Bryant's Minstrels, was first performed in New York in 1859 and published the following year. It was written as a rousing walk around with banjos ringing and bones rattling while members of the cast sang, danced, and pranced in review.

It was not a patriotic song, but it was claimed by the South early in the Civil War as its theme song. A band played it at the Confederate inauguration of President Jefferson Davis, and it became a regional favorite. At Appomattox, President Lincoln requested a band to play it as a measure of his approval and in recognition of the return of the southern states to the union. As time has passed, the tune has been heard more often in instrumental arrangements than in vocal adaptations. The words of the verses are no longer heard because they are nonsensical and racially offensive. Among later composers who have incorporated "Dixie" is New Englander Charles Ives.

Written by the comedian Harry McCarthy, "The Bonnie Blue Flag" (No. 112) was eclipsed in popularity only by "Dixie" among Southerners. It was set to the tune "The Irish Jaunting Car," but it was the text that made it a favorite throughout the wars. Southerners were called gallant, valorous, and brave patriots. The flag with the single white star was praised. Reference to Northern treachery declared the bias. Rancorous Northern parodies immediately appeared, naming Southerners rebels, traitors, deceivers, tyrants, cunning, false advisers, and vandals with barbaric spirits. Death was threatened both to the ghastly serpent flag and to the wretches over whom it waved.

The frequency with which he heard the southern version of this song so irritated Major General Benjamin Butler, who commanded Union armies occupying New Orleans, that he banned it in 1862. He arrested and fined A. E. Blackmar, its publisher, the sum of $500.00. He also threatened to levy a fine of $25.00 on any man, woman, or child who sang, played, or even whistled it. In the twentieth century a southern college fraternity adopted it as its theme song, but the text no longer represented southern sentiments and the music setting was too frail to endure.

Critics were baffled as to why "Weeping Sad and Lonely" (No. 113) became one of the most popular Civil War songs. They judged both the poetry and music to be mediocre. Singers both north and south, however, had instincts that went beyond rationality. In four brief verses, the sentiments were of courtly love, patriotism, nostalgia, and religiosity. Lost hope, the fear of being wounded, and dying alone were deeply felt emotions even by those who remained at home. The music that enhanced these basic feelings was lyric, direct, and singable. The mystery of the song's success cannot not be discovered through technical analysis of either the poetry or the music. The answer probably lies in the perfect fitting of the rhythm of the poetry to the music, the moderate vocal range, the brevity of the phrases, and the plaintive melodic lines. As with many other songs of the period, parodies and answer-songs followed its publication both in the Union states and the Confederacy. Washington M. Ives, Jr., of Live Oak volunteered for duty with the Confederate army. He survived fierce battles and wrote letters to members of his family during his term of service. From a camp near Chattanooga in 1863 he wrote to his mother: "Our brass band is the best in this army. It has been playing a piece which Katie [his sister] plays, 'The Switzer's Farewell'." "The Switzer's Farewell" (No. 114) combined sad memories and a yodel. The song of homesickness evoked memories of tranquil times and a desire to return to an untroubled life. It was a familiar emotion that had been sung by the Irish and African Americans. William Austin relates this sentiment to the song "Old Folks at Home."

Many songs about the war lost their popularity just as the Confederacy lost the war. A few battle pieces sustained the grief of families of slain soldiers in gray, but the most enduring songs were love songs. A favorite in the South was "Lorena" (No. 115). This ballad is about a love that prospered once in youth but later became only an unforgettable memory. The final verse promises that the lovers will meet again after death. This song was in the repertoire of the Florida Fourth Regimental band during the Civil War.

"Come into the Garden, Maud!" (No. 116) was written by Otto Dresel, an excellent composer and pianist who was a pupil of Hiller and Mendelssohn. He wrote art songs similar in style to those of Robert Franz. His texts were from Tennyson, Longfellow, and Oliver Wendell Holmes. Dresel was "beloved as an artist and dreaded as a critic," according to Julia Ward Howe. He was a leader of the cultural community in Boston in the 1850s and 1860s. He shared the views of his patron John Sullivan Dwight and wrote articles for *Dwight's Journal of Music*. He had no tolerance for democracy and wrote that only a refined and cultured audience could or should be allowed to appreciate the *best* music. The song included here illustrates both his appeal and his textbook craftmanship. It is included in only one Florida collection.

A bound music collection belonging to Evelyn Byrd Cameron, a Monticello pianist, is now in the music library of Florida State University. It contains many titles that remain in present-day repertory as well as a few that lost their appeal by the end of the nineteenth century. Among the piano pieces are first editions of the Waltz in C-sharp Minor (No. 117) and Beethoven's Moonlight Sonata, Op. 27. For voice are selections from *Sicilian Vespers, Ernani, Il Trovatore, Un Ballo in Maschera,* and *L'Eclair* and two part-songs by Mendelssohn. Included here is "Preghiera," from Verdi's *Un Ballo in Maschera* (No. 118), an aria sung by Adelia in the opera and by aspiring sopranos in Monticello.

Louis Moreau Gottschalk was born in New Orleans in 1829. When he was thirteen, his parents sent him to Paris. He made his debut as a pianist and composer at the Salle Pleyel when he was twenty. It took only three years for him to conquer Europe: the French, the Swiss, the Spanish, Chopin, Liszt, Berlioz, the public, and the critics. An astonished writer for *La France Musicale* wrote "a Creole composer, bon Dieu." Gottschalk returned to the United States in 1853 and mesmerized American audiences with both his virtuosity and his personal charisma. He traveled from coast to coast, giving 1,100 concerts. Later, he attained celebrity in the Caribbean and South America. Critics decried his excesses, but audiences delighted in the unique style of his exotic dances and the impassioned grace of his sentimental keyboard works. Florida pianists could not resist an artist who was also a matinee idol. Mary Laura Call, grandmother of Mary Call Collins, played Gottschalk's "Forest Glade Polka" (No. 119), Op. 25 (1853) in J. C. Viereck's four-hand arrangement, and her copy of the score is in the Florida Agricultural and Mechanical University archives. Bound in the same volume are several dances: polkas, mazurkas, quadrilles, and an arrangement of themes from *Il Trovatore* by Ferdinand Beyer. "Ojos Criollos" (No. 120), Op. 37, a lively Cuban dance, was one of three Gottschalk works in the libraries of both Evelyn Byrd Cameron of Monticello and Mary Laura Call. The four-hand version was published in Boston by Oliver Ditson. It captivated audiences in Havana and Europe as well as in North America. Gottschalk wrote that he intended to capture the singular rhythm and charming character of Creoles in the Spanish Antilles. The popularity of this piece indicated that he achieved his goal, though later writers have failed to agree on the name of the strong rhythmic patterns. One called them cakewalk and Habañera, another called them a polka-tango.

They do agree that he was a brilliant pianist. His compositions epitomized the romantic style. The public gave them applause and responded as groupies to a matinee idol. Florida pianists conformed to the tastes of the nation. They applauded the genius of Gottschalk as a style setter of syncopation, shifting harmonies, tremolos, and arpeggios that stretched across the keyboard. Gottschalk used these techniques in quoting Stephen Foster's "Camptown Races" and the spiritual "Roll Jordan, Roll." The vigor of his use of rhythm may be heard in both "Ojos Criollos" and "Forest Glade Polka." His gift for transforming indigenous dance tunes into popular music for the salon or recital hall anticipated events of our own century. His style by any measurement was extravagant. It has returned in many forms over the years, and he has become a luminary among American keyboard composers.

I have written about the purposes and functions of music as groups moved in and out of Florida. I have not limited my perspective to music that invites aesthetic contemplation. For the most part, our music was social or work communication. It grew out of the experiences of the people who made it. The Native Americans sang songs of thanksgiving at festivals in the spring and autumn. The Spanish brought soaring Catholic chant and counterpoint. The French preferred unison song tunes at their Protestant services. A distinguishing feature of early Florida music was the manifold changes that it accommodated as it passed through generations of national groups. Early settlers from five continents brought music of their cultures, and some of it survives in the twentieth century. For this book I have chosen examples from the rich matrix of our heritages. They are vivid reminders of life and times in early Florida: the setting, the people, their uses of music, their taste, and their style.

103. Alice Gray

WILLIAM MEE

MRS. P. MILLARD

She's all my fan - cy pain - ted her, She's love - ly, she's di -

vine;_____ But her heart it is an - oth - er's, She nev - er can be mine; Yet

lov'd I as man nev - er lov'd, A love with - out de - cay,_____ Oh! my heart, my heart is

break - ing For the love of A - lice Gray! Oh! my heart, my heart is break- ing For the

love of A - lice Gray!

2.
Her dark brown hair is braided
　O'er a brow of spotless white;
Her soft blue eye now languishes,
　Now flashes with delight:
Her hair is braided not for me,
　The eye is turned away;
Yet my heart, my heart is breaking
　For the love of Alice Gray.

3.
I've sunk beneath the summer sun,
　And trembled in the blast;
But my pilgrimage is nearly done,
　The weary conflict's past:
And when the green sod wraps my grave,
　May pity haply say, —
"Oh! his heart, his heart is broken
　For the love of Alice Gray."

2.
Her dark brown hair is braided
　O'er a brow of spotless white;
Her soft blue eye now languishes,
　Now flashes with delight:
Her hair is braided not for me,
　The eye is turned away;
Yet my heart, my heart is breaking
　For the love of Alice Gray.

3.
I've sunk beneath the summer sun,
　And trembled in the blast;
But my pilgrimage is nearly done,
　The weary conflict's past:
And when the green sod wraps my grave,
　May pity haply say, —
"Oh! his heart, his heart is broken
　For the love of Alice Gray."

104. Oft in the Stilly Night

THOMAS MOORE

1.Oft in the stil - ly night, Ere slum - ber's chain has bound me,
2.When I re - mem - ber all The friends, so link'd to - geth - er,
D. C.— Thus in the stil - ly night, Ere slum - ber's chain has bound me,

Fond mem - 'ry brings the light Of oth - er days a - round me. The
I've seen a - round me fall, Like leaves in win - try weath - er, I
Sad mem - 'ry brings the light Of oth - er days a - round me.

smiles, the tears Of boy - hood's years, The words of love then spo - ken. The
feel like one Who treads a - lone Some ban - quet hall de - sert - ed, Whose

eyes that shone, Now dimm'd and gone, The cheer - ful hearts now bro - ken!
lights are fled, Whose gar - lands dead, And all but he de - part - ed.

105. Cheer! Boys, Cheer!

CHARLES MACKAY

HENRY RUSSELL

1

Cheer! boys, cheer! no more of idle sorrow,
Courage, true hearts shall bear us on our way;
Hope points before and shows the bright to-morrow,
Let us forget the darkness of to-day:
So, farewell, England, much as we may love thee,
We'll dry the tears that we have shed before.
Why should we weep to sail in search of fortune?
So farewell, England, farewell for evermore!
Cheer! boys, cheer! for country, mother country,
Cheer! boys, cheer! the willing strong right hand:
Cheer! boys, cheer! there's wealth for honest labour!
Cheer! boys, cheer! for the new and happy land.

2

Cheer! boys, cheer! the steady breeze is blowing,
To float us freely o'er the ocean's breast.
The world shall follow in the track we're going;
The star of empire glitters in the west.
Here we had toil and little to reward it,
But there shall plenty smile upon our pain;
And ours shall be the prairie and the forest,
And boundless meadows ripe with golden grain.
Cheer! boys, cheer! for country, mother country
Cheer! boys, cheer! united heart and hand;
Cheer! boys, cheer! there's wealth for honest labour!
Cheer! boys, cheer! for the new and happy land.

106. Kathleen Mavourneen

bright   dew is shak - ing,   Kath-leen   Ma - vour-neen,   what! slum - b'ring

still?   Oh!   hast   thou for-

Espress. e legato

got-ten   how   soon   we must sev-er,   Oh   hast   thou for-got-ten,   this

Kath - leen Ma - vour - neen, a - wake from thy slum-bers, The blue moun-tains glow in the Sun's gol-den light. Ah! where is the spell that once hung on my num-bers? A - rise in thy beauty, thou

star of my night! A - rise in thy beau - ty, thou star of my night.

Tempo 1 ^{mo}

Slentando

Con Amore affetto

mf

Ma - vour - neen, Ma - vour-neen, my

Rallent.

f

mf

fz

mf

sad tears are fal - ling, To think that from E - rin and thee I must part! It

may be for years, and it may be for-ev-er, Then why art thou si - lent? thou

mp

Sempre legato

mf *Semplice mf* *mf* *mf*

voice of my heart, It may be for years, and it may be for - ev- er, Then

mf

why art thou si - lent? Kath-leen Ma - vour-neen!

Rallent. *dim.* *e piano*

107. Old Folks at Home

STEPHEN COLLINS FOSTER

Way down up-on de Swa-nee rib-ber, Far, far a-way, Dere's wha my heart is turn-ing eb-ber, Dere's wha de old folks stay. All up and down de whole cre-a-tion,

2d Verse.
All round de lit-tle farm I wan-dered, When I was young, Den man - y hap - py days I squan-dered, Man - y de songs I sung. When I was play-ing wid my brud-der, Hap - py was I, Oh! take me to my kind old mud-der, Dere let me live and die.

CHORUS

3d Verse.
One lit - tle hut a - mong de bush-es, One dat I love, Still sad - ly to my mem-'ry rush-es, No mat - ter where I rove. When will I see de bees a - hum-ming All round de comb? When will I hear de ban-jo tum-ming Down in my good old home?

CHORUS

108. Come Where My Love Lies Dreaming

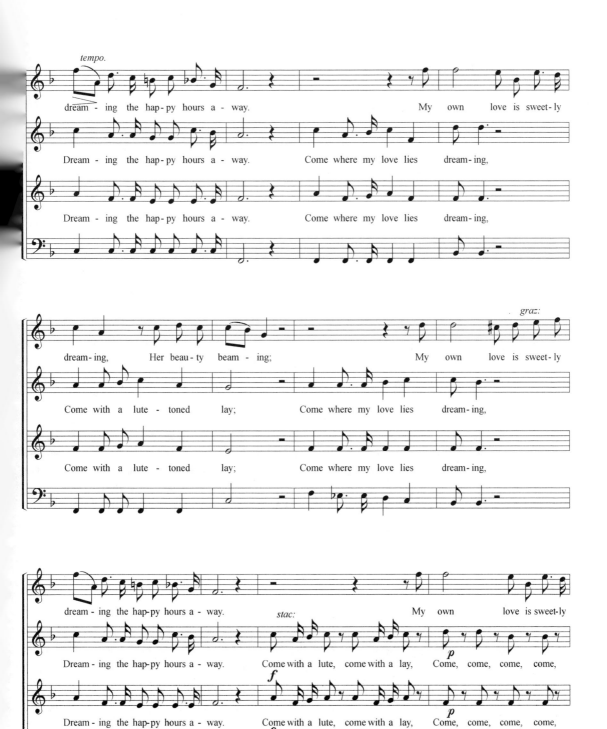

109. Listen to the Mocking Bird

ALICE HAWTHORNE
(SEPTIMUS WINNER)

I'm dream-ing now of Hal - ly, sweet Hal - ly, sweet Hal - ly; I'm
Ah! well I yet re - mem - ber, re - mem - ber, re - mem - ber, Ah!

dream - ing now of Hal - ly, For the thought of her is one that nev - er dies: She's
well I yet re - mem- ber, When we ga - ther'd in the cot - ton side by side: 'Twas

sleep - ing in the val - ley, the val - ley, the val - ley; She's
in the mild Sep - tem- ber, Sep - tem- ber, Sep - tem- ber, 'Twas

sleep - ing in the val - ley, And the mock- ing bird is sing-ing where she lies.
in the mild Sep - tem- ber, And the mock- ing bird was sing-ing far and wide.

CHORUS

SOLO

Lis-ten to the mock- ing bird, Lis-ten to the mock- ing bird, The mock-ing bird still sing-ing o'er her

3

When the charms of spring awaken,
And the mocking bird is singing on the bough,
I feel like one forsaken,
Since my Hally is no longer with me now.

110. Wait for the Wagon

R. P. BUCKLEY

Will you come with me, my Phyl-lis dear, to yon Blue Moun-tain free. Where blos-soms smell the sweet-est, come rove a-long with me; It's ev-'ry Sun-day morn-ing, when I am by your side, We'll jump in-to the wag-on and all take a ride. Wait for the wag-on, wait for the wag-on, Wait for the

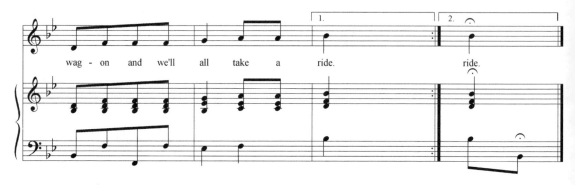

wag - on and we'll all take a ride. ride.

2.

Where the river runs like silver
And the birds they sing so sweet,
I have a cabin, Phyllis,
And something good to eat;
Come listen to my story,
It will relieve my heart;
So jump into the wagon,
And off we will start.
CHORUS

3.

Do you believe, my Phyllis dear,
Old Mike, with all his wealth,
Can make you half so happy
As I, with youth and health?
We'll have a little farm,
A horse, a pig, and cow;
And you will mind the dairy
While I do guide the plough.
CHORUS

4.

Your lips are red as poppies,
Your hair so slick and neat,
All braided up with dahlias,
And hollyhocks so sweet.
It's ev'ry Sunday morning,
When I am by your side,
We'll jump into the wagon,
And all take a ride.
CHORUS

5.

Together, on life's journey,
We'll travel till we stop,
And if we have no trouble,
We'll reach the happy top;
Then come with me, sweet Phyllis,
My dear, my lovely bride,
We'll jump into the wagon,
And all take a ride.
CHORUS

111. Dixie's Land

Daniel D. Emmett

take my stand, To lib and die in Dix - ie, A - way, A - way, A - way down south

Dix - ie, A - way, A - way, A - way down south in Dix - ie.

Ole missus marry "Will de weaber,"
Willium was a gay deceaber;
Look away! Look away! Look away! Dixie Land.
But when he put his arm around 'er,
He smiled as fierce as a forty pounder,
Look away! Look away! Look away! Dixie Land.
Chorus

His face was sharp as a butcher's cleaber,
But dat did not seem to greab 'er;
Look away! Look away! Look away! Dixie Land.
Ole missus acted de foolish part,
And died for a man dat broke her heart,
Look away! Look away! Look away! Dixie Land.
Chorus

Now here's a health to the next old Missus,
An' all de gals dat want to kiss us;
Look away! Look away! Look away! Dixie Land.
But if you want to drive 'way sorrow,
Come and hear dis song tomorrow,
Look away! Look away! Look away! Dixie Land.
Chorus

Dar's buckwheat cakes and Injun batter,
Makes you fat or a little fatter;
Look away! Look away! Look away! Dixie Land.
Den hoe it down an scratch your grabble,
To Dixie's Land I'm bound to trabble,
Look away! Look away! Look away! Dixie Land.
Chorus

112. The Bonnie Blue Flag

HARRY McCARTHY

Irish Traditional melody

We are a band of bro-thers, and na-tive to the soil, Fight-ing for the prop-er-ty we gained by hon-est toil; And when our rights were threat-ened, the cry rose near and far: "Hur-rah for the Bon-nie Blue Flag that bears a sin-gle star!"

Hur - rah! Hur - rah! for South - ern rights, hur - rah! Hur -

rah for the Bon - nie Blue Flag that bears a sin - gle star!

As long as the Union was faithful to her trust;
Like friends and brethren kind were we, and just;
But now, when Northern treachery attempts our rights to mar,
We hoist on high the Bonnie Blue Flag that bears a single star.
Chorus

Ye men of valor gather round the banner of the right,
Texas and Louisiana join us in the fight;
With Davis, our loved President, and Stephens, statesmen rare,
We'll rally round the Bonnie Blue Flag that bears a single star.
Chorus

Then here's to our Confederacy, strong we are and brave,
Like patriots of old we'll fight, our heritage to save;
And rather than submit to shame, to die we would prefer,
So cheer for the Bonnie Blue Flag that bears a single star.
Chorus

First gallant South Carolina nobly made the stand,
Then came Alabama and took her by the hand;
Next, quickly, Mississippi, Georgia, and Florida,
All raised on high the Bonnie Blue Flag that bears a single star.
Chorus

And here's to brave Virginia, the Old Dominion State,
With the young Confederacy at length has linked her fate;
Impelled by her example, now other States prepare
To hoist on high the Bonnie Blue Flag that bears a single star.
Chorus

Then cheer, boys, cheer, raise a joyous shout,
For Arkansas and North Carolina, now have both gone out,
And let another rousing cheer for Tennessee be given,
Then single star of the Bonnie Blue Flag has grown to be eleven.
Chorus

113. Weeping Sad and Lonely (when This Cruel War is Over)

CHARLES C. SAWYER

HENRY TUCKER

Dear - est love, do you re - mem - ber When we last did meet,

How you told me that you loved me, Kneel - ing at my feet?

Oh! how proud you stood be - fore me, In your suit of blue,

When the summer breeze is sighing,
Mournfully along;
Or when autumn leaves are falling,
Sadly breathes the song.
Oft in dreams I see thee lying
On the battle plain.
Lonely, wounded, even dying,
Calling but in vain.
Chorus

If amid the din of battle,
Nobly you should fall,
Far away from those who love you,
None to hear your call,
Who would whisper words of comfort,
Who would soothe your pain?
Ah! the many cruel fancies
Ever in my brain.
Chorus

But our country called you, darling,
Angels cheer you on your way;
While our nation's sons are fighting,
We can only pray.
Nobly strike for God and liberty,
Let all nations see,
How we love the starry banner,
Emblem of the free.
Chorus

114. The Switzer's Farewell

George Linley

Adieu   dear   land,   With beau - ty   teem - ing,   Where first I
Von mei - ne   Ber - ge muss i   stei - ge   wo's   gar so

rov'd   a   care - less   child;   Of   thee   my   heart   Will e'er be   dream - ing,   Thy   snow - clad
lieb - lich   ist   und   schön   kann nim - mer   in   der Hei - math   blei - be   muss   doch zum

peaks and moun - tains wild. Dear land! That I cher - ish, Oh, long may'st thou
Diend't noch - mal gehn Jo li o li_

flour - ish; My mem' - ry must per - ish, Ere I for - get thee.

Far from my home I soon must wan - der, In stran - ger
B'hu - et di Gott mei lie - be En - gel gieb mir no

land be doom'd to dwell. O! best be - loved! My heart grows fond - er, While thus I

a mal die Hand gar lang wirst mi ja mim - ma seh'n denn i roas

breathe my last fare - well. Re - ceive this sad to - ken, I leave thee, heart bro - ken, Our

in a fren - des Land Jo li o li_

part - ing is spo - ken, Be lov'd one! fare - well.

115. Lorena

H.D.L. Webster

J.P. Webster

The years creep slow-ly by, Lo - re - na; The snow is on the grass a-

gain; The sun's low down the sky, Lo - re - na; The frost gleams where the flow-ers have

been. But the heart throbs on as warm-ly now As when the sum-mer days were

nigh; Oh! the sun can nev-er dip so low.. A - down af - fec-tion's cloud-less sky.

A hundred months have passed, Lorena,
Since last I held that hand in mine,
And felt the pulse beat fast, Lorena,
Though mine beat faster far than thine.
A hundred months--t'was flowery May.
When up the hilly slope we climbed,
To watch the dying of the day
And hear the distant church bells chime.

We loved each other then, Lorena,
More than we ever dared to tell;
And what we might have been, Lorena,
Had but our loving prospered well!
But then, 'tis past: the years have gone,
I'll not call up their shadowy forms;
I'll say to them, "Lost years, sleep on,
Sleep on, nor heed life's pelting storms."

116. Come into the Garden, Maud!

ALFRED, LORD TENNYSON.

OTTO DRESEL.

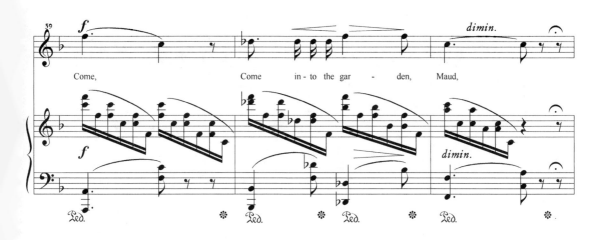

Come,   Come   in - to the gar - den,   Maud,

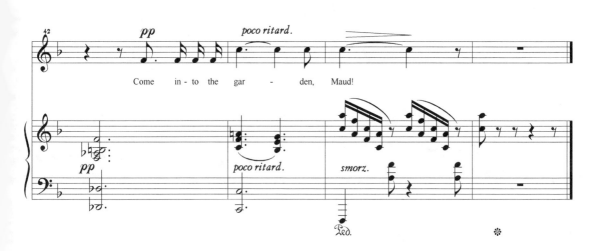

Come   in - to   the   gar - den,   Maud!

117. Waltz in C-sharp Minor

Tempo giusto.

FRÉDÉRIC CHOPIN.

118. Preghiera, from *Un Ballo in Maschera*

mi - o, l'u-ni-co fi - glio mio av-vin-cere al mio se - no

E seal-la mo - glie nie - ghi quest' ul - ti-mo fa - vor,

non ri - fiu-tar - loai prie - ghi, ai prie - ghi del mio ma - ter no

cor.   Mor - rò, ma que - ste vi - sce - re con-

so - li - noi suoi ba - ci,   or che l'es - tre - maè

giun - ta   dell' o - re mi - e fu - ga - ci...

Spen - ta per man del pa - dre, la man ei sten - de -
rà su gl'oc - chi d'u - na ma - dre, su gl'oc - chi d'u - na
mad - re, che mai più non ve - drà, che mai più, mai più, che mai più non ve -

A Masked Ball (Verdi)
Act II, Scene I
Amelia:
I shall die, but first, in mercy,
Grant at least that I may hold against my breast
My only son, my only son.
If you deny a wife this last request,
Do not deny the prayers, the prayers of a mother's heart.

I shall die, but let my sorrow
Be comforted by his kisses
Now that the last of my fleeting hours has come!
Though she was slain by the father's hand,
The son will reach for the eyes of his mother,
Who never again will see him.
Ah! who never again will see him!

119. Forest Glade Polka

LOUIS MOREAU GOTTSCHALK,
arranged for Piano 4 Hands by
J.C. VIERECK.

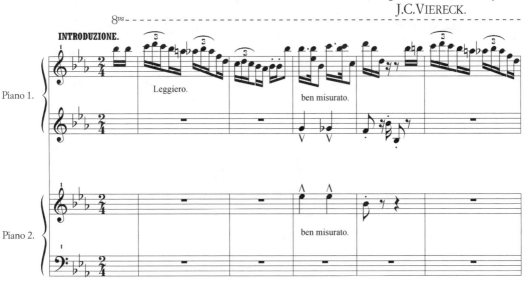

POLKA.

BRILLANTE.

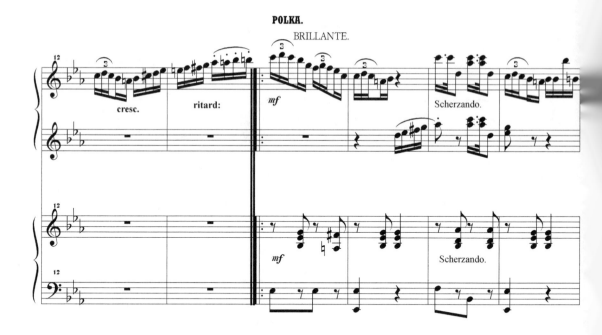

TRANQUILLAMENTE MA CON ANIMA.

120. Ojos Criollos

L.M. Gottschalk

AN ANTHOLOGY OF MUSIC IN EARLY FLORIDA

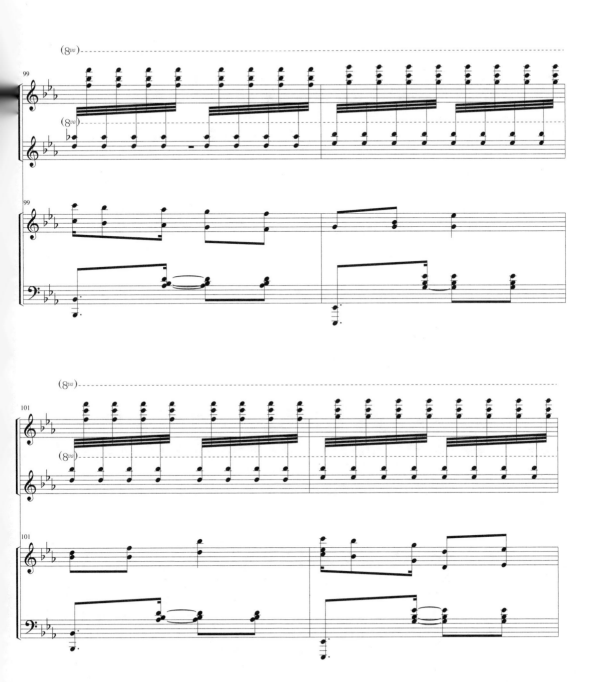

Sources

CHAPTER 1: THE NATIVE AMERICANS

NO. 1   "Ball Game Dance." Frank G. Speck, *Ceremonial Songs of the Creek and Yuchi Indians.* University of Pennsylvania Anthropological Publications, vol. 1, no. 2, 182–83. Philadelphia: University Museum, 1911.

NO. 2   "Quail Dance." Albert Gale, Minnie Moore-Willson, "The Seminole Indians of Florida." *Florida Historical Society Quarterly* 7, no. 1 (July 1928), 81–84, 154–58.

NO. 3   "Chicken Dance." Albert Gale, Minnie Moore-Willson, "The Seminole Indians of Florida." *Florida Historical Society Quarterly* 7, no. 1 (July 1928), 81–84, 154–58.

NO. 4   "Hunting Dance Song." Albert Gale, Minnie Moore-Willson, "The Seminole Indians of Florida." *Florida Historical Society Quarterly* 7, no. 1 (July 1928), 81–84, 154–58.

NO. 5   "Corn Dance Song." Frances Densmore, *Seminole Music.* Smithsonian Institution, U.S. Bureau of American Ethnology, Bulletin 161, p. 56. Washington, D.C.: U.S. Government Printing Office, 1956.

NO. 6   "The Death of Osceola." B. F. Baker. Boston: Henry Rolman, 1846.

CHAPTER 2: THE SPANISH

NO. 7   "Ave Maria." *Liber Usualis,* ed. Benedictines of Solesmes, p. 575. New York: Desclee, 1963.

NO. 8   "Vexilla Regis." *Liber Usualis,* ed. Benedictines of Solesmes, p. 1857. New York: Desclee, 1963.

NO. 9   "The Litany of Loreto." *Liber Usualis,* ed. Benedictines of Solesmes, p. 1861. New York: Desclee, 1963.

NO. 10   "La Generala." *Toques de Guerra,* arr. R. P. N. Otaño and D. Manuel de Espinosa, pp. 1–3. Burgos: Radio Nacional de España, 1939.

NO. 11   "El Bando." *Toques de Guerra,* arr. R. P. N. Otaño and D. Manuel de Espinosa, p. 23. Burgos: Radio Nacional de España, 1939.

NO. 12   "Diferencias sobre el 'Canto del Cavallero'." Antonio de Cabezón, *Obras de Musica para tecla, arpa, y vihuela.* Barcelona: Instituto Español de Musicologia, 1966.

NO. 13   "Al amor quiero vencer" (Villancico NO. 7). Luis de Milán, *El Maestro*, ed. Charles Jacob, p. 254. University Park: Pennsylvania State University Press, 1971.

NO. 14   "Pavan NO. 4." Luis de Milán, *El Maestro*, ed. Charles Jacob, p. 105. University Park: Pennsylvania State University Press, 1971.

CHAPTER 3: THE FRENCH

NO. 15   "Psalm 130." Claude Goudimel and Clément Marot, *Claude Goudimel oeuvres complètes*, 9:132. New York: Institute of Medieval Music, 1967.

NO. 16   "Psalm 137." Claude Goudimel and Clément Marot, *Claude Goudimel oeuvres complètes*, 9:249. New York: Institute of Medieval Music, 1967.

NO. 17   "Psalm 128." Claude Goudimel and Clément Marot, *Claude Goudimel oeuvres complètes*, 9:130. New York: Institute of Medieval Music, 1967.

NO. 18   "Psalm 5." Claude Goudimel and Clément Marot, *Claude Goudimel oeuvres complètes*, 9:5. New York: Institute of Medieval Music, 1967.

CHAPTER 4: THE BRITISH

NO. 19   "Grenadier's March." T. S. St. Clair, *A Residence in the West Indies and America* (1834), 1:2. Quoted by Lewis Winstock in *Songs and Music of the Redcoats*, p. 90. London: Leo Cooper, 1970.

NO. 20   "The Duke of York's March." As performed by his Royal Highness's new band in the Coldstream Regiment of Guards. London: T. Skillern, n.d. No composer designated. Adopted by the King's Royal Rifles (Sixteenth Foot). See John Farmer, *Scarlet and Blue* (London: Cassell, 1896), 14.

NO. 21   "Rule Britannia." Thomas Arne, *National, Patriotic, and Typical Airs of All Lands*, arr. John Philip Sousa, p. 118. New York: DaCapo, 1987.

NO. 22   "Five Variations on the National Air." L. Van Beethoven. London: Preston, n.d.

NO. 23   "Dead March from *Saul*." G. F. Handel. New York: J. Hewitt, 1804.

NO. 24   "Roslin Castle." James Johnson and William Stenhouse, *The Scots Musical Museum*, 1:9. Edinburgh: Reprinted by Folklore Associates, Hatboro, Penn., 1962.

NO. 25   "The Princess of Hess's Minuet." *Rutherford's Compleat Collection of the Most Celebrated Minuets*, 2:11. London, 1775–80.

NO. 26   "Lady Augusta's Minuet." *Rutherford's Compleat Collection of the Most Celebrated Minuets*, 2:56. London, 1775–80.

NO. 27   "The Duchess of Richmond's Minuet." *Rutherford's Compleat Collection of the Most Celebrated Minuets*, 2:12. London, 1775–80.

NO. 28   "Balendalloch's Dream." *The Complete Repository of Original Scots Tunes, Strathspeys and Dances, First Part*, p. 9. Edinburgh: Neil Gow and Sons, 1799.

NO. 29   "Go to the Devel and Shake Yourself." *The Complete Repository of Original Scots Tunes, Strathspeys, Jigs and Dances, Part Second*, p. 21. Edinburgh: Neil Gow and Sons, 1802.

NO. 30 "The Marquis of Huntley's Strathspey." William Marshall, *The Complete Repository of Original Scots Tunes, Strathspeys, Jigs and Dances, Part Second*, p. 9. Edinburgh: Neil Gow and Sons, 1802.

NO. 31 "The Star." *Thompson's Compleat Collection of 200 Favourite Country Dances*, 1:91. London: Charles and Samuel Thompson, 1760. Reprint, 1770–80.

NO. 32 "Shuter's Humour." *Thompson's Compleat Collection of 200 Favourite Country Dances*, 1:65. London: Charles and Samuel Thompson, 1760. Reprint, 1770–80.

NO. 33 "Her Mouth, Which a Smile." From *Rosina*. William Shield, in *A Miscellaneous Collection . . . in Two Volumes*, 1:139. London: Fred. Aug. Hyde, 1798.

NO. 34 "This Cold, Flinty Heart." From *Cymon*. Michael Arne, in *A Miscellaneous Collection . . . in Two Volumes*, 1:31. London: Fred. Aug. Hyde, 1798.

NO. 35 "Within This Breast the Record Lies." From *The Flitch of Bacon*. William Shield, in *A Miscellaneous Collection . . . in Two Volumes*, 1:170. London: Fred. Aug. Hyde, 1798.

NO. 36 "No, 'Twas Neither Shape nor Feature." J. C. Bach. From *The Flitch of Bacon*. William Shield, in *A Miscellaneous Collection . . . in Two Volumes*, 1:139. London: Fred. Aug. Hyde, 1798.

CHAPTER 5: MILITARY MEN AND PATRIOTS

NO. 37 "Hail to the Chief." *Heart Songs*, ed. Joe Mitchell Chapple, p. 440. Boston: Chapple Publishing Co., 1909.

NO. 38 "The Cruiskeen Lawn," *Folksongs of England, Ireland, Scotland and Wales*, eds. William Cole and Norman Monath, pp. 62–63. New York: Charles Hansen, 1961.

NO. 39 "Rude Boreas," *Shanties and Sailors' Songs*, Stan Hugill, pp. 158–59. New York: Frederick A. Praeger Publishers, 1969.

NO. 40 "President Jackson's Grand March," J. T. Norton. Philadelphia: G. E. Blake, n.d.

NO. 41 "Before Jehovah's Awful Throne." Lowell Mason, *The Boston Handel and Haydn Society Collection of Church Music*, pp. 215–19. New York: DaCapo Press, 1973.

NO. 42 "Within a Mile of Edinburgh," Peter Urbani, arr., *A Selection of Scots Songs*, pp. 50–51. Edinburgh: Author, 1794.

NO. 43 "Landlord, Fill the Flowing Bowl," *Heart Songs*, ed. Joe Mitchell Chapple, p. 141. Boston: Chapple Publishing Co., 1909.

NO. 44 "The Hunters of Kentucky," New York: T. Birch, 1824.

NO. 45 "Come, Haste to the Wedding." *The Elopement*, T. Giordani. A pantomime from *The Duenna* by Thomas Linley, *English Theatre in the Eighteenth Century*, p. 410. London, 1775.

NO. 46 "Wondrous Love." B. F. White and E. J. King, *The Sacred Harp*, p. 159. Nashville: Broadman, 1859. Facsimile edition, 1962.

NO. 47 "Amazing Grace." B. F. White and E. J. King, *The Sacred Harp*, p. 262. Nashville: Broadman, 1859. Facsimile edition, 1962.

NO. 48 "When I Can Read My Title Clear." Isaac Watts. B. F. White and E. J. King, *The Sacred Harp*, p. 58. Nashville: Broadman, 1859. Facsimile edition, 1962.

NO. 49 "Easter Anthem." B. F. White and E. J. King, *The Sacred Harp*, p. 235. Nashville: Broadman, 1859. Facsimile edition, 1962.

NO. 50 "Awake, My Soul, Stretch Every Nerve." *The Boston Handel and Haydn Society Collection of Sacred Music*, ed. Lowell Mason. Boston: Richardson and Lord, 1822, p. 128. Reprint, *Earlier American Music*, NO. 15. New York: DaCapo Press, 1973.

NO. 51 "Mighty God, Eternal Father." *The Boston Handel and Haydn Society Collection of Sacred Music*, ed. Lowell Mason. Boston: Richardson and Lord, 1822, p. 203. Reprint, *Earlier American Music*, NO. 15. New York: DaCapo Press, 1973.

NO. 52 "Come, Thou Almighty King." *The Boston Handel and Haydn Society Collection of Sacred Music*, ed. Lowell Mason. Boston: Richardson and Lord, 1822, p. 33. Reprint, *Earlier American Music*, NO. 15. New York: DaCapo Press, 1973.

NO. 53 "A Great Camp-meetin' in de Promised Land." Mrs. M. F. Armstrong and Helen Ludlow, *Hampton and Its Students*, p. 222. New York: G. P. Putnam's Sons, 1874.

NO. 54 "I'm a-Rolling." J. B. T. Marsh, *The Story of the Jubilee Singers with Their Songs*, p. 9. Boston: Houghton, Mifflin, 1880.

NO. 55 "Good News, de Chariot's Comin'." T. F. Seward, *Religious Folk Songs of the Negro*, p. 52. Hampton: The Institute Press, 1920.

NO. 56 "Mary and Martha." T. F. Seward, arr., *The Jubilee Singers*, p. 210. Boston: Lee and Shepard, 1873.

CHAPTER 7: FOLK SINGERS AND DANCERS

NO. 57 "Roll Jordan, Roll." James Weldon Johnson and J. Rosamond Johnson, *The Book of American Spirituals*, pp. 105–7. New York: DaCapo Press, 1969.

NO. 58 "Didn't It Rain, My Elder." Charles L. Edwards, *Bahama Songs and Stories*, p. 25. New York: G. E. Stechert and Co., 1942. Reprint, 1976.

NO. 59 "Git on Board." Charles L. Edwards, *Bahama Songs and Stories*, p. 26. New York: G. E. Stechert and Co., 1942. Reprint, 1976.

NO. 60 "Sich a Gitting Up Stairs." Lester S. Levy, *Grace Notes in American History*, pp. 89, 92–93. Baltimore: G. Willig, Jr., 1967.

NO. 61 "Jordan Am a Hard Road to Travel." Piano Duet. Charles Grobe. Boston: Oliver Ditson, 1854.

NO. 62   "Jock O'Hazeldean." Josiah Pittman and Colin Brown, *Songs of Scotland*, p. 9. London: Boosey, 1877.

NO. 63   "My Boy Tammy." Scottish Ballad. *Ladies Musical Library* 2 (February 1843), 25.

NO. 64   "The Birks of Invermay." Peter Urbani, arr., *A Selection of Scots Songs*, pp. 32–33. Edinburgh: Author, 1794.

NO. 65   "Good Night and Joy Be Wi' Ye." George Thompson, *A Select Collection of Original Scottish Airs*, 4:200. Edinburgh: G. Thompson, 1803.

NO. 66   "Barbara Allan." George Thompson, *A Select Collection of Original Scottish Airs*, 3:130. Edinburgh: G. Thompson, 1803. Florida State University Music Library, Whitfield Collection (hereafter Whitfield Collection).

NO. 67   "The Exile of Erin." Thomas Campbell, *Our Familiar Songs*, p. 91. New York: Arno Press, 1974.

NO. 68   "Roll the Cotton Down." Stan Hugill, *Shanties from the Seven Seas*, p. 154. London: Routledge and Kegan Paul, 1961.

NO. 69   "Clear the Track." Stan Hugill, *Roll and Go*, p. 43. Indianapolis: Bobbs-Merrill, 1924.

NO. 70   "John, Come Tell Us as We Haul Away." Stan Hugill, *Shanties from the Seven Seas*, p. 287. London: Routledge and Kegan Paul, 1961.

NO. 71   "Sir Roger de Coverley." Mari Ruef Hofer, *Polite and Social Dances*, p. 43. Chicago: Clayton F. Summy, 1917.

NO. 72   "The Forked Deer." R. P. Christeson, *Old-time Fiddler's Repertory*, p. 89. Columbia: University of Missouri Press, 1973.

NO. 73   "Fisher's Hornpipe." R. P. Christeson, *Old-time Fiddler's Repertory*, p. 57. Columbia: University of Missouri Press, 1973.

NO. 74   "Leather Breeches." R. P. Christeson, *Old-time Fiddler's Repertory*, p. 123. Columbia: University of Missouri Press, 1973.

NO. 75a   "Green Gravel." Cecil J. Sharp, arr., *Children's Singing Games*, p. 18, Set V. London: Novello, 1912.

NO. 75b   "Green Gravel." English, arr., Florida African American Children. In "Ring Plays and Other Games of the Florida Negro," Grace Fox, D.P.E. diss., Indiana University, 1949.

NO. 76   "Shule Agra." Margaret Bradford Boni and Norman Lloyd, *The Fireside Book of Favorite American Songs*, p. 342. New York: Simon and Schuster, 1952.

NO. 77   "Robin Adair." Margaret Bradford Boni and Norman Lloyd, *The Fireside Book of Favorite American Songs*, p. 342. New York: Simon and Schuster, 1952.

NO. 78   "The Girl I Left Behind Me." J. C. Viereck. Macon: J. C. Schreiner, n.d.

CHAPTER 8: THE SOCIAL CIRCLE

NO. 79   "Florida Schottish." G. Torrente. New York: William Hall and Son, 1852.

NO. 80   "Florida." Theod. Von La Hache. New York: Firth, Pond and Co., 1854.

NO. 81   Overture from *Il Tancredi*. Gioacchino Rossini. Amsterdam: Edition Compusic, 1988.

NO. 82   "La Trènis." Jean Schneitzhoffer, *La Sylphide*. Charles Jarvis, arr., *Ladies Musical Library*, 1:75, n.d.

NO. 83a   "L'Eté." D. F. E. Auber, *Le Dieu et la Bayadère*. Baltimore: G. Willig, Jr., 1836.

NO. 83b   "La Pantalon." D. F. E. Auber, *Le Dieu et la Bayadère*. Baltimore: G. Willig, Jr., 1836.

NO. 83c   "Brahma." D. F. E. Auber, *Le Dieu et la Bayadère*. Baltimore: G. Willig, Jr., 1836.

NO. 84   "Katy-Did Polka." Louis Antoine Jullien. New York: William Hall and Son, 1855.

NO. 85   "Cally Polka." Allen Dodworth, arr. New York: Firth, Hall and Pond Co., 1846.

NO. 86   "The Hope Waltzes." B. Hope. Baltimore: John Cole, n.d.

NO. 87   "Jim Crow." T. D. Rice, *Series of Old American Songs*. Providence: Brown University Library, 1936.

NO. 88   "Home, Sweet Home." Henry R. Bishop. Philadelphia: George Bacon, 1823.

NO. 89   "Echo Song." Henry R. Bishop. Boston: Oliver Ditson, n.d.

NO. 90   "Near the Lake Where Drooped the Willow." Charles E. Horn. New York: Hewitt and Jacques, 1839.

NO. 91   "Hope Told a Flatt'ring Tale." Giovanni Paisiello, *Lady Cushington Collection*. London: F. A. Hyde, n.d.

NO. 92   "The Harper's Song." T. V. Wiesenthal. Baltimore: George Willig, n.d.

NO. 93   "My Home, My Happy Home." G. A. Hodson. Philadelphia: Lee and Walker, n.d.

NO. 94   "Schlaf wohl, du süsser Engel du!" Franz Abt, Op. 213, NO. 3. Philadelphia: G. André, n.d.

NO. 95   "Er ist gekommen." Robert Franz. Boston: Oliver Ditson, 1903.

NO. 96   "Camptown Races." Stephen C. Foster. Baltimore: F. D. Benteen, 1852.

NO. 97   "Nelly Bly." Stephen C. Foster. New York: Firth, Pond and Co., 1849.

NO. 98   "Beautiful Dreamer." Stephen C. Foster. New York: William A. Pond, 1862.

NO. 99   "Zip Coon." G. W. Dixon. New York: J. L. Hewitt Co., n.d.

NO. 100   "Wood Up Quick Step." John Holloway Blanchor, arr. Philadelphia: G. E. Blake, n.d.

NO. 101   "Switzer's Song of Home." German folksong. J. Moschelles. Louisville: D. P. Faulds, n.d.

NO. 102   "Nothing Else To Do." J. L. Hatton. Boston: Oliver Ditson, n.d.

CHAPTER 9: THE MEN IN GRAY AND THE FOLKS AT HOME

NO. 103   "Alice Gray." Mrs. P. Millard, *The Songs of England*. 3 vols., arr. J. L. Hatton and Easton Fanning, 1:158. New York: Boosey and Co., n.d.

NO. 104   "Oft in the Stilly Night." Thomas Moore, *Heart Songs*, p. 91. New York: DaCapo Press, 1983.

NO. 105 "Cheer! Boys, Cheer!" Henry Russell, *The Oxford Song Book*, coll. and arr. Percy C. Buck. London: Humphrey Milford, 1924.

NO. 106 "Kathleen Mavourneen." P. N. Crouch. Columbia, S.C.: George Dunn and Co, n.d.

NO. 107 "Old Folks at Home." Stephen C. Foster. New York: Firth, Pond and Co., 1851.

NO. 108 "Come Where My Love Lies Dreaming." Stephen C. Foster. New York: Firth, Pond and Co., 1855.

NO. 109 "Listen to the Mocking Bird." Septimus Winner (Alice Hawthorne). Thomas Marrocco and Harold Gleason, *Music in America*, p. 318. New York: W. W. Norton, 1964.

NO. 110 "Wait for the Wagon." R. P. Buckley. Paul Glass and Louis C. Singer, *Singing Soldiers*, p. 44. St. Louis: Educational Publisher, 1964.

NO. 111 "Dixie's Land." Daniel Emmett. Boston: Oliver Ditson, 1860.

NO. 112 "The Bonnie Blue Flag." Harry McCarthy. New Orleans: Blackmar, 1861.

NO. 113 "Weeping Sad and Lonely." Henry Tucker. Irwin Silber, *Songs of the Civil War*, p. 124. New York: Columbia University Press, 1960.

NO. 114 "The Switzer's Farewell." George Linley. New York: Firth, Pond and Co., n.d.

NO. 115 "Lorena." J. P. Webster. Chicago: H. M. Higgins, 1857.

NO. 116 "Come into the Garden, Maud!" Otto Dresel. Boston: Russell and Telman, n.d.

NO. 117 "Waltz in C-sharp Minor." Frederick Chopin. Berlin: A. M. Schlesinger, 1837.

NO. 118 "Preghiera." G. Verdi, *Un Ballo in Maschera*. Paris: Leon Escudier, n.d.

NO. 119 "Forest Glade Polka." Louis Moreau Gottschalk. Boston: Oliver Ditson, 1853.

NO. 120 "Ojos Criollos." Louis Moreau Gottschalk. New York: William Hall and Son, 1864.

Selected Bibliography

Allen, William Francis, Charles Pickard Ware, and Lucy McKim Garrison. *Slave Songs of the United States*. New York: A. Simpson, 1867. Reprint, New York: Oak Publications, 1965.

Armstrong, Mrs. M. F., and Helen W. Ludlow. *Hampton and Its Students*. New York: G. P. Putnam's Sons, 1874.

Auber, D. F. E. *Quadrilles from "Le Dieu et la Bayadère."* Baltimore: G. Willig, Jr., 1836.

Austin, William W. "Susanna," "Jeanie," and "The Old Folks at Home." New York: Macmillan, 1975.

Ballentine, George. *Autobiography of an English Soldier in the United States Army*. New York: Stringer and Townsend, 1853.

Benzoni, Girolamo. *Histoire nouvelle du Nouveau Monde*. Geneva: Apud Eustace Vignon, 1579. Appended with half-title "Brief discours et histoire d'un voyage de quelques Francois en la Floride [by Nicolas Le Challeux, from the account first published in Dieppe, 1566].

Boni, Margaret Bradford, and Norman Lloyd, *The Fireside Book of Favorite American Songs*. New York: Simon and Schuster, 1952.

Bronson, Bertrand Harris. *The Traditional Tunes of the Child Ballads*. 2 vols. Princeton: Princeton University Press, 1962.

Broyles, Michael. *Music of the Highest Class*. New Haven: Yale University Press, 1992.

Buck, Percy C. *The Oxford Song Book*. London: Oxford University Press, 1924.

Cabezón, Antonio de. *Obras de Musica para tecla, arpa, y vihuela*. Barcelona: Instituto Espagñol de Musicologia, 1966.

Camus, Raoul F. *Military Music of the American Revolution*. Chapel Hill: University of North Carolina Press, 1976.

Cash, William Thomas. "Taylor County History." *Florida Historical Quarterly* 27, no. 1 (July 1948): 28–58.

Catholic Hymnal and Service Book. New York: Benziger Editions, 1966.

Chappell, William. *Old English Popular Music*. New York: Jack Brussel, 1961.

Chapple, Joe M. *Heart Songs*. Boston: Chappel Publishing Co., 1909. Reprint, New York: DaCapo Press, 1983.

Chase, Gilbert. *America's Music*. New York: McGraw-Hill, 1955. Revised edition, Urbana: University of Illinois Press, 1987.

Christeson, R. P. *Old-time Fiddler's Repertory*. Columbia: University of Missouri Press, 1973.

Clio and Euterpe; or, British Harmony. Vol. 1. London: Henry Roberts, 1762.

Curtis Burlin, Natalie. *Hampton Series of Negro Folk Songs*. New York: G. Schirmer, 1918–19.

Damon, S. Foster. *Series of Old American Songs*. Facsimile. Providence: Brown University Press, 1936.

Davis, William Watson. "The Civil War and Reconstruction in Florida." Ph.D. diss., Columbia University, 1913.

Dean, Winton. *Handel's Dramatic Oratorios and Masques*. London: Oxford University Press, 1959.

Densmore, Frances. *Seminole Music*. Smithsonian Institution, U.S. Bureau of American Ethnology, Bulletin 161. Washington, D.C.: U.S. Government Printing Office, 1956.

Dolph, Edward Arthur. *Sound Off!* New York: Cosmopolitan Book, 1929.

Dorman, George H. *Fifty Years Ago: Reminiscences of 1861–1865*. Tallahassee: T. J. Appleyard, 1912.

Douen, O. *Clément Marot et le psautier Huguenot*. 2 vols. Paris: À l'Imprimerie Nationale, 1878.

Edwards, Charles L. *Bahama Songs and Stories*. Boston: Houghton, Mifflin, 1895.

Eppes, Susan Bradford. *The Negro of the Old South*. Chicago: Joseph G. Branch Publishing, 1925.

Fairbanks, George R. *The History and Antiquities of St. Augustine, Florida*. New York: Norton, 1858; Jacksonville: H. Drew, 1881. Reprint, Gainesville: University Presses of Florida, 1975.

Farmer, John. *Scarlet and Blue*. London: Cassell, 1896.

Fiske, Roger. *English Theatre Music of the Eighteenth Century*. London: Oxford University Press, 1973.

Ford, Ira W. *Traditional Music of America*. New York: DaCapo Press, 1978.

Foster, Stephen C. *Foster Hall Reproduction of Songs*. Indianapolis: Josiah Kirby Lilly, 1932.

Fox, Grace. "Ring Plays and Other Games of the Florida Negro." D.P.E. diss., Indiana University, 1949.

Funk, Joseph. *New Harmonia Sacra*. 22nd edition. Shenandoah Valley: Harmonia Sacra Singing Movement, 1959.

Gammond, Peter. *The Oxford Companion to Popular Music*. Oxford: Oxford University Press, 1991.

Glass, Paul, and Louis C. Singer. *Singing Soldiers*. New York: Grosset and Dunlop, 1964, 1968. Reprint, New York: DaCapo Press, 1975.

Gomme, Alice Bertha. *The Traditional Games of England, Scotland, and Ireland*. 2 vols. London: David Nutt, 1898.

Gow, Niel. *Complete Repository of Original Scots Tunes, Strathspeys, and Dances*. Edinburgh: Gow and Shepherd, 1802.

Gravier, Gabriel, ed. *Deuxième voyage du dieppois Jean Ribaut à la Florida en 1565*. Rouen: Imprimerie de Henry Boissel, 1872.

Grobe, Charles. *Favorite Melodies*. Boston: Oliver Ditson, 1854. (Includes "Jordan Am a Hard Road," four hands.)

Hamm, Charles, ed. *Music in the New World*. New York: W. W. Norton, 1982.

——. *Yesterdays: Popular Song in America*. New York: W. W. Norton, 1979.

Harwell, Richard Barksdale. *Songs of the Confederacy*. New York: Broadcast Music, 1951.

Hatton, J. L., and Eton Faning. *Songs of England*. London: Boosey, 1900.

Heaps, Willard A., and W. Porter Heaps. *The Singing Sixties*. Norman: University of Oklahoma Press, 1960.

The Home Circle. Vol. 1. Boston: Oliver Ditson, 1859. Reprint, New York: DaCapo Press, 1983.

Hughes, John. "The Tientos, Fugas, and Diferencias in Antonio de Cabezón's 'Obras de Musica Para tecla, Harpa y Vihuela'." Ph.D. diss., Florida State University, 1961.

Hugill, Stan. *Shanties and Sailors' Songs*. New York: Praeger, 1969.

——. *Shanties from the Seven Seas*. London: Routledge and Kegan Paul, 1961.

Jackson, Richard, ed. *Popular Songs of Nineteenth-Century America*. New York: Dover, 1976.

Johnson, H. Earle. *Operas on American Subjects*. New York: Coleman-Ross, 1964.

Johnson, James, and William Stenhouse. *The Scots Musical Museum*. Hatboro, Penn.: Folklore Associates, 1962.

Kinsey, Terry L. *Songs of the Seas*. London: Robert Hale, 1989.

Klemm, Eberhard, ed. *Louis Moreau Gottschalk Kreolische und Karibische Klavierstucke*. Leipzig: Edition Peters, 1974.

Lawrence, Vera Brodsky. *The Piano Works of Louis Moreau Gottschalk*. New York: Arno Press and New York Times, 1969.

Levy, Lester S. *Grace Notes in American History: Popular Sheet Music from 1820–1900*. Norman: University of Oklahoma Press, 1967.

Liber Usualis. Edited by the Benedictines of Solesmes. New York: Desclee, 1963.

List, Eugene. *Gottschalk: A Compendium of Piano Music*. New York: Carl Fischer, 1971.

Long, Ellen Call. *Florida Breezes*. 1882. Reprint, Gainesville: University of Florida Press, 1962.

Marsh, J. B. T. *The Story of the Jubilee Singers*. Boston: Houghton, Mifflin, 1880.

Mason, Lowell, ed. *The Boston Handel and Haydn Society Collection of Church Music*. Boston: Richardson and Lord, 1822.

McCall, George A. *Letters from the Frontiers*. 1868. Reprint, Gainesville: University Presses of Florida, 1974.

Milán, Luis de. *El Maestro*. University Park: Pennsylvania State University Press, 1971.

Morris, Alton C. *Folksongs of Florida*. Gainesville: University of Florida Press, 1950.

Moore, Thomas. *National Airs*. Boston: O. Ditson, 1893.

Morocco, W. Thomas, and Harold Gleason. *Music in America*. New York: W. W. Norton, 1964.

Nathan, Hans. *Dan Emmett and the Rise of Early Negro Minstrelsy*. Norman: University of Oklahoma Press, 1962.

Nelson, Robert U. *The Technique of Variation*. Berkeley: University of California Press, 1949.

Norton, J. T. *President Jackson's Grand March*. Philadelphia: G. E. Blake, n.d.

One Thousand Fiddle Tunes. Chicago: M. M. Cole, 1940.

Opie, Iona, and Peter Opie. *The Singing Game*. New York: Oxford University Press, 1985.

Otaño, R. P. N., and D. Manuel de Espinosa. *Toques de Guerra*. Burgos: Radio Nacional de España, 1939.

Pedrell, Filipe. *Anthology of Classical Spanish Organists*. Vols. 1–2. New York: Associated Music Publishers, 1905.

Pidoux, Pierre. *Le psautier Huguenot du seizième siècle*. 2 vols. Bale: Barenreiter, 1962.

Pike, G. D. *The Jubilee Singers*. Boston: Houghton, Mifflin, 1880.

Pittman, Josiah. *Songs of Scotland: A Collection of One Hundred and Ninety Songs*. London: Boosey, 1879.

Porter, Susan. *With an Air Debonair*. Washington, D.C.: Smithsonian Institution Press, 1991.

Quadrilles from "Le Dieu et la Bayadère." New York: Hewitt and Jacques, n.d.

Root, Dean L. *Music of Florida Sites*. Tallahassee: Florida State University, 1983.

Rutherford's Compleat Collection of the Most Celebrated Minuets. 2 vols. London, 1775–80.

Rutherford's Compleat Collection of Two Hundred of the Most Celebrated Country Dances. 2 vols. London, 1756–60.

Sharp, Cecil J., and Maud Karpeles. *English Folk Songs from the Southern Appalachians*. 2 vols. London: Oxford University Press, 1932.

Silber, Irwin. *Songs of the Civil War*. New York: Columbia University Press, 1960.

Shipp, John. *The Path of Glory: Being the Memoirs of the Extraordinary Military Career of John Shipp*. London: Chattus and Windus, 1969.

Smith, Julia Floyd. *Slavery and Plantation Growth in Antebellum Florida, 1821–1860*. Gainesville: University of Florida Press, 1973.

Sonneck, O. G. *Early Opera in America*. New York: Benjamin Blom, 1963. Original Sonneck copyright, 1915.

Sousa, John Philip. *National, Patriotic, and Typical Airs of All Lands*. Philadelphia, 1890. Reprint, New York: DaCapo Press, 1977.

Speck, Frank G. *Ceremonial Songs of the Creek and Yuchi Indians*. University of Pennsylvania Anthropological Publications, vol. 1, no. 2. Philadelphia: University Museum, 1911.

Thompson, Charles, and Samuel Thompson. *Thompson's Compleat Collection of Two Hundred Favourite Country Dances*. 4 vols. London: Charles and Samuel Thompson, 1760. Reprint, 1770–80.

Thompson, George. *A Select Collection of Original Scottish Airs*. Vols. 2, 4. London: T. Preston, 1803–16.

Thompson, William. *Orpheus Caledonius*. 2 vols. London: Author, 1733.

Urbani, Peter. *A Collection of Scots Songs*. 2 vols. Edinburgh: Urbani and Liston, 1792.

Watts, Isaac. *Hymns and Spiritual Songs*. Exeter, N.H.: John I. Williams, 1822.

White, Benjamin Franklin, and E. J. King. *The Sacred Harp*. Nashville: Broadman Press, 1968.

Winstock, Lewis. *Songs and Music of the Redcoats*. London: Leo Cooper, 1970.